# LLOYD GEORGE

*and the Liberal Dilemma*

**MICHAEL LYNCH**

Hodder & Stoughton
LONDON SYDNEY AUCKLAND

**Acknowledgments**

The publishers would like to thank the following for their kind permission to reproduce illustrations in this volume;

National Portrait Gallery, London cover. Punch Publications, p. 5, p. 45, p. 84. Gwynedd Culture & Leisure: Archives & Museums p. 34, p. 46, p. 111. The Hulton-Deutsch Picture Company p. 48.

The publishers would also like to thank the following for permission to reproduce material in this volume; Longman Group UK for the extract from *Lloyd George*, M. Pugh, 1988.

Every effort has been made to trace and acknowledge ownership of copyright. The publishers will be glad to make suitable arrangements with any copyright holders whom it has not been possible to contact.

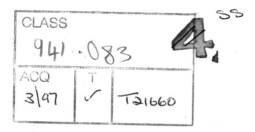
**British Library Cataloguing in Publication Data**
Lynch, Michael
  Lloyd George and the Liberal Dilemma. –
  (Personalities & Powers Series)
  I. Title  II. Series
  941.083092
  ISBN 0-340-56317-6

First published 1993
Impression number   10   9   8   7   6   5   4   3   2   1
Year                     1998   1997   1996   1995   1994   1993

Typeset by Litho Link Ltd, Welshpool, Powys, Wales.
Printed in Great Britain for the educational publishing division of Hodder and Stoughton Ltd, Mill Road, Dunton Green, Sevenoaks, Kent by St Edmundsbury Press, Bury St Edmunds.

# CONTENTS

# INTRODUCTION

## LIFE AND TIMES

David Lloyd George once described how, during a train journey through a valley in his native Wales, he was struck by the way the quality of the female underwear hanging out to dry changed as he went up the line. He observed that at the bottom of the valley, where the poorest cottages were situated, the women's underclothing was made of cotton, wool or calico. At the top of the valley, where the best homes were, the maidservants were pegging out the satins, silks and lace of their well-to-do mistresses. Lloyd George declared that he looked forward to the time when every woman in the valley would be able to wear the underclothes of her choice; until that day came Britain could not count herself a fair or free society. In that homely, if slightly risqué description, is typified Lloyd George's attitude towards privilege and social inequality and his ability to choose striking ways of putting across his political message.

David Lloyd George is the only British Prime Minister not to have spoken English as his first language. His native tongue was Welsh, and his Welshness was an essential part of his make-up as a politician. He represented the Welsh constituency of Caernarvon Boroughs without a break from 1890 to 1944. In doing this he won 13 consecutive election victories, making him one of the longest-serving members of Parliament in British political history.

His long service is only one aspect of his remarkable career. If his Welshness remained an indelible feature of his character, it is as an outstanding national politician and a renowned international statesman that Lloyd George is best remembered. The period of 55 years during which he was in politics was one of the most dramatic and significant in modern British history. Of the many major issues of that time there was scarcely one in which Lloyd George was not involved. In peace and in war, he was to be found in the forefront of national affairs. It should come as no surprise, therefore, to learn that his prolonged involvement in public affairs occasioned intense controversy during his lifetime and continuing historical debate since. Lloyd George was the type of person towards whom it was difficult to feel indifference; he seemed to inspire either affection or loathing.

It is a commonplace of historical observation that every period is one of transition. However, there are particular grounds for applying that term to the years during which Lloyd George was active in politics. Between 1890 and 1945, a period dominated by two world wars, Britain underwent a social, economic and political transformation on a scale sufficient, in the eyes of some historians, to merit the description 'revolution'.

This book is not intended as a biography of Lloyd George. It is an attempt to survey the key aspects of his career as a way of illustrating the great issues of his time. By examining Lloyd George's career, one is involved in studying the major issues confronting Britain in the last decades of the nineteenth century and the first half of the twentieth century. Particular attention is paid to the years 1905 and 1922, since that is the most critical period in Liberal Party fortunes and the time when Lloyd George was at his most influential.

## THE LIBERAL DILEMMA

The two major political parties of late Victorian Britain were the Liberals and the Conservatives (at this time more usually referred to as Unionists because of their opposition to the granting of Irish Home Rule and their support of the Act of Union between Britain and Ireland). In government, each party had introduced social reform legislation, but important though these measures were, they were inadequate to cope with the economic and social problems created by industrialisation. What was needed was a far greater commitment to reform, a plan comprehensive enough to tackle the difficulties on a national scale. Those who argued for such an undertaking were known as radicals. The radical faction within the Liberal Party wanted the adoption of social reform policies that would both deal with the economic problems and appeal to the growing working class, which, with the widening of the franchise after the Reform Bills in 1867 and 1884-5, was becoming an ever-growing electoral force. Such pressure created a dilemma for the Liberal Party. It became faced with a crisis of identity.

Under its greatest nineteenth-century exponent, W.E. Gladstone, who continued to dominate his party until his death in 1898, Liberalism had become a movement essentially concerned with tackling the great moral issues of the day, such as the Anglo-Irish and the Eastern questions. Gladstone defined party as 'an instrument for the attainment of great ends'. The modern historian, Peter Clarke, describes Gladstone's brand of Liberalism as 'moral populism'. Consumed as he was by these great moral crusades, Gladstone had neglected to give his full attention to British social problems. This had frustrated the radicals in his party; the split over Home Rule in 1886 therefore had been the occasion rather than the cause of the breakup of the old Liberal Party. The Liberal radicals argued that the priorities with which the party should be concerning itself were the 'bread and butter' domestic issues of social and economic deprivation and the mass poverty that nineteenth-century industrialisation had brought in its wake. They regarded Gladstone's programme of 'peace, retrenchment and reform', associated with the high tide of Liberalism in the 1870s, as no longer relevant in the age of mass politics that had come to characterise the final Victorian decades. Gladstone's reluctance to change and his longevity eventually led many radicals to decide to leave the Party.

This encouraged the industrial workers and the trade unions that represented them to doubt that the Liberal Party could genuinely represent their interests; the result was a strong movement towards the idea of an entirely separate political party, dedicated to advancing the cause of the workers. The outcome was the amalgamation in 1900 of a variety of radical groups into the Labour Representation Committee, the forerunner of the Labour Party of 1906. The Liberals' failure to make themselves the party of the working class meant that once the Labour Party had come into being it was difficult for them to claim that they were a genuinely radical party. That role had been usurped by the new Labour Party. Although it was not their intention, the Liberals found themselves pushed by circumstances into occupying the middle-ground between Labour and the Conservatives.

This did not happen immediately; it took some time before the young

Labour Party was able to mount a serious electoral challenge to the Liberals. Indeed, in its early days the Labour Party saw its best means of exerting an influence to lie in co-operating with the Liberals. It was this understanding that produced the Lib-Lab pact, an agreement made in 1903 between Ramsay MacDonald and Herbert Gladstone, the respective chief whips of the Labour and Liberal parties, that their candidates would not compete against each other in parliamentary constituencies. Nevertheless, the implications were clear. The Liberals now had a rival; should they fail to meet the social and economic challenges of the time, there was a radical force waiting to supersede them.

The Liberals' problem was dramatised by the career of the outstanding radical in the party, Joseph Chamberlain. Despairing of the apparent inability of a party led by Gladstone ever being able to adapt itself to the real needs of the nation, Chamberlain took the dramatic step in the late 1880s of abandoning the Liberals and joining the Unionists. His decision was motivated in part by his anger at Gladstone's attempt to grant Home Rule to Ireland, but he was equally concerned to advance his own particular schemes for dealing with national poverty. Chamberlain was fearful that if the plight of the industrial masses was left untouched they would turn to revolutionary socialism and plunge Britain into violent class warfare. In 1885 he challenged his leader, Gladstone, by presenting his own radical 'Unauthorised Programme', advocating an extensive scheme of social reform. Chamberlain explained the principles behind his programme in these terms:

> Politics is the science of human happiness, and the business of a statesman and of politicians is to find out how they can raise the general condition of the people; how they can increase the happiness of those who are less fortunate among them. What are the facts of the case? I sometimes think that we are so used to poverty and to its consequences that we forget it or neglect it. Yet surely there is some reason to doubt the perfection of our system when in this, the richest country in the world, one in thirty of the population at every moment are unable to obtain the means of subsistence without recourse to the parish [a system of relief], and one in ten at the same time are on the verge of starvation.

## FORCED FELLOWSHIP.

SUSPICIOUS-LOOKING PARTY. "ANY OBJECTION TO MY COMPANY, GUV'NOR? I'M AGOIN' YOUR WAY "—(aside) "AND FURTHER."

Chamberlain went further. His solution was to develop the British Empire into an economic federation through the use of preferential tariffs (a modern parallel would be the European Community, though he took the USA as his model), the profits from which would be directed into alleviating social distress in Britain. Having broken from the Liberal Party in the late 1880s, he joined the Conservatives and set about persuading his new party to adopt his scheme of tariff reform as their official economic policy.

The significance of Chamberlain's behaviour is that it highlighted one of the crucial trends of the time, the growing political importance of working-class issues. The development of mass membership trade unions was a feature of this. Out of trade unionism grew the plan for a distinct political party that could genuinely represent the interests of the unions and the working class. Some historians, notably Peter Clarke, suggest that this marks the beginning of 'class' politics in Britain; the suggestion being that the awareness of the working class of its own potential became the most significant factor in electoral politics.

Chamberlain was Lloyd George's first great political hero. Sharing Chamberlain's dislike of socialism he, too, wished to pre-empt its rise and believed this could best be achieved by the Liberal Party's widening its political appeal by adopting social reform as its major political objective. In this respect, Lloyd George was a representative of what has become known as the 'New Liberalism' of the period. The term refers to the change that came in Liberal thinking around the turn of the century. In response to the increasingly evident social and economic problems, many Liberals began to move away from the older form of Liberal thought which had given only a limited role to the State in the improvement of social conditions. Old Liberalism may be conveniently summarised under the Gladstonian slogan 'Peace, Retrenchment and Reform'. 'Peace' referred to the belief that Britain should avoid war and unnecessary foreign entanglements by embracing the concepts of internationalism and anti-imperialism. 'Retrenchment' was the idea of saving public money by tightly controlling central-government expenditure. 'Reform' allowed for necessary changes to be introduced by government, but, since the chief characteristic of the older variety of Liberalism was its emphasis on individual freedom, it restricted government-led reform to the redress of outstanding grievances. It certainly did not intend that the State should undertake a comprehensive programme of social and economic reform.

For the new Liberals this brand of Liberalism had been made obsolete by the rapidly changing social conditions in Britain. They argued that the progressive elements in traditional Liberalism should be expanded to embrace the new situation. An important voice in the formulation of new liberal thinking was J.A. Hobson. Writing in 1909, he summed up the essential change of attitude.

Liberalism is now formally committed to a task which certainly involves a new conception of the State in its relation to the individual life and to private enterprise. That conception is not Socialism in any accredited meaning of that term, though implying a considerable amount of increased public ownership and control of industry. From the standpoint which best presents its continuity with earlier Liberalism, it appears as a fuller appreciation and realisation of individual liberty contained in the provision of equal opportunities for self-development. But to this individual standpoint must be joined a just apprehension of the social, *viz.*, the insistence that these claims or rights of self-development must be adjusted to the sovereignty of social welfare.

What Hobson is claiming here is that, in effect, Gladstonian Liberalism is dead. What Liberalism now represents, he suggests, is an acceptance that social welfare is a paramount policy. Liberty and freedom of enterprise remain valid objectives, but they must take second place to what is essentially a moral purpose. The rights of the individual must not be pursued at the expense of the general social good. Equal opportunity ought now to be the goal of Liberal policies. This requires that the State extend its authority to encompass social reform. Hobson specifically denies that what he is proposing is a form of socialism; rather it is the creation of the social-service state (a concept which later analysts have described as a halfway stage between the high Liberalism of the nineteenth century and the welfare state of the twentieth century).

In a time of rapid transition existing institutions come under pressure; they either adapt successfully or become obsolete. The essential question facing the Liberal Party in the early decades of the twentieth century was whether it could modify its ideas and structure sufficiently to enable it to continue as an effective force in British politics. The changes in society and economy that were taking place presented it with a series of challenges to its philosophy and traditions. In British politics the record suggests that a party must have flexibility and adaptability in order to survive. Those parties that have lacked such qualities have withered or died, no matter how strong their original beliefs may have been.

The dilemma facing the Liberal Party was this; should it stand fast to its principles at the risk of being overtaken by events and becoming politically redundant, or should it modernise itself in such a way as to remain progressive but at the cost of its original motivation. It is a question with which all political parties are confronted at some point in their development; it was the Liberal Party's particular fate that it should meet the question during the half-century that coincided with the parliamentary career of Lloyd George. His impact upon the development of the Liberal Party in particular and on British politics in general is the theme of this book.

# 2

# THE POLITICAL AGENDA

In order to understand the problems that made up the political agenda in Lloyd George's time, it is necessary to describe the essential changes that were taking place in late Victorian and Edwardian Britain and the political issues to which they gave rise.

## THE PROBLEM OF POVERTY

The early decades of Lloyd George's life witnessed a remarkable and unprecedented growth in the size and the concentration of the British population. This was the era of the growth of towns and the formation of the great conurbations. The table below, taken from the 1911 Census, indicates the dimensions and location of this development:

**TABLE I**

|      | Greater London | South East Lancashire | West Midlands | West Yorkshire | Merseyside |
|------|----------------|-----------------------|---------------|----------------|------------|
| 1871 | 3 890 000      | 1 386 000             | 969 000       | 1 064 000      | 690 000    |
| 1901 | 6 856 000      | 2 117 000             | 1 483 000     | 1 524 000      | 1 030 000  |
| 1911 | 7 256 000      | 2 328 000             | 1 634 000     | 1 590 000      | 1 157 000  |

These figures strikingly illustrate the phenomenal growth in the conurbations of industrial Britain. In the 40 years after 1871, the population in those areas had virtually doubled. Even if sophisticated welfare services had been available, the sheer scale of the increase would have been difficult to contain. In the event, the rudimentary character of such welfare schemes as did exist, together with the lack of adequate physical resources in such areas as water supply, sanitation and housing rendered the burdens insurmountable. Overcrowding, malnutrition and ill-health, everpresent problems throughout the nineteenth century, were intensified. The Poor Law, the only major welfare scheme in operation, had been introduced in an earlier age when it was believed that poverty could be contained by dealing with it on a local basis, parish by parish. However, the enormous increase in population made this system of parish relief wholly inadequate to deal with the problem.

The grim poverty that shaped the lives of the mass of people who lived in the towns and cities was graphically revealed in a series of definitive public reports. Outstanding pioneering studies were produced by Charles Booth and Seebohm Rowntree; their meticulously-detailed analysis of social conditions in London and Yorkshire respectively gave evidence of appalling squalor and deprivation.

> Life in Class A. Income under 18s. weekly for a moderate family. Three examples of cases considered within this group:
> 1. No occupation. Married. Aged sixty-four. Two rooms. The man has 'not had his boot on' for twelve months. He is suffering from dropsy. His wife cleans schools. This house shares one closet [WC] with eight other houses, and one water tap with four others. Rent 2s. 6d. [13p.] . . .
> 2. Out of work. Married. Four rooms. Five children, Drinks. 'Chucked his work over a row'. Very poor; has to pawn furniture to keep his children. Rent 4s. [20p.] . . .
> 3. Widow. Four rooms. One baby. Semi-lunatic family. Receives Poor Relief. Son, who is wage earner, is weak bodily and mentally. Ditto the daughter. Nice house, but dirty. 4s. [20p.] per week is received for an illegitimate child being brought up here. This house shares one closet with another house, and one water tap with three other houses.
> 
> . . . we are faced by the startling probability that from 25 to 30 per cent of the town populations of the United Kingdom are living in poverty.
> 
> In this land of abounding wealth, during a time of perhaps unexampled prosperity, probably more than one fourth of the population are living in poverty . . ., There is surely need for

greater concentration of thought by the nation upon the well-being
of its own people, for no civilization can be sound or stable which
has at its base this mass of stunted human life.

(from Seebohm Rowntree, *Poverty: A Study of Town Life*, 1901)

Such were the worst effects of the uncontrolled industrial growth of
Victorian Britain. The stark details of the nation's urban blight, which
were now being systematically gathered and published, provided
evidence of a degree of social deprivation that politicians could not
ignore. Debate was sharpened and parties were forced to come to grips
with the implications. The crisis of identity in the Liberal Party,
highlighted since 1886 by the breakaway of Joseph Chamberlain, was
intensified. The Conservatives were similarly faced with the need to
develop a relevant social policy; one of their major responses was to
adopt Chamberlain's economic protectionist policies, which were based
on the notion that by operating a system of tariff reforms and imperial
preference, Britain could raise surplus capital to spend on social reform.
The presence after 1900 of a parliamentary Labour Party, although
initially small in number and limited in influence, was further evidence
that working class issues were beginning to shape the political agenda.

The irrefutable evidence of widespread poverty and distress posed a
number of demanding and overlapping questions. What should be the
response of Government and Parliament? Were the central and local
authorities directly responsible for dealing with the problem? How
extensive were the powers of the State to be and how could these be
reconciled with the rights and freedoms of the individual citizen? Did the
State have the right to encroach upon the lives of the people even if it was
intended for their own good? Should the traditional *laissez-faire*, hands-
off, approach be replaced by Government-directed social welfare
policies? These were particularly demanding questions for the Liberals,
by tradition the party that championed the principle of the freedom of
the individual. The Liberal dilemma had been clearly expressed in 1885
in an exchange between Gladstone, the Liberal leader, and Joseph
Chamberlain following the issuing by the latter of his Unauthorised
Programme, a radical challenge to the leader's official Liberal policy.
Chamberlain spoke of:

Squalid homes, unhealthy dwellings, overcrowding; these are the
causes of the crime and immorality of great cities. They are the

direct result of a system which postpones the good of the community to the interest of individuals, which loses sight altogether of the obligations of property in a servile adulation of its rights.

Gladstone responded by saying:

The [radical] Liberalism of today is far from being good. Its pet idea is what they call construction – that is to say, taking into the hands of the state the business of the individual man.

## FREE TRADE VERSUS PROTECTION

As the graph on page 13 shows, Britain's trade and industry appeared to be shrinking, relative to other countries, such as Germany and the United States. Between 1870 and 1914 the British industrial growth rate of 2.3 per cent was only half that of the United States. By the turn of the century Germany and the USA had overtaken Britain in the volume of their iron and steel production. By 1910, British industrial exports made up only 10 per cent of the world trade compared with figures of 20 per cent for German goods and 40 per cent for American. Modern revisionist historians have argued that the decline was exaggerated by contemporaries who were unnecessarily frightened by the growth of Germany and the USA. As they argue it, the truth was that 'in absolute terms' British industry was still growing and was more productive (i.e., cost effective) than American and German industry even though total output in those two countries was higher. The revisionists insist that it was the First World War which caused Britain's twentieth-century industrial decline by shattering the international economy in which Britain had held such a predominant place.

However, no matter how strongly the revisionists may now press their case, it has to be emphasised that, at the time, the late Victorian and Edwardian industrialists genuinely believed that the trade figures showed that they could not compete with their American and German rivals in the open market. The insistent economic question of the day was, therefore, should the Government abandon the traditional policy of free trade, which had been successful in the middle years of the century when Britain had held a substantial industrial lead, in favour of a policy of protection, involving the imposition of tariffs and regulations, aimed

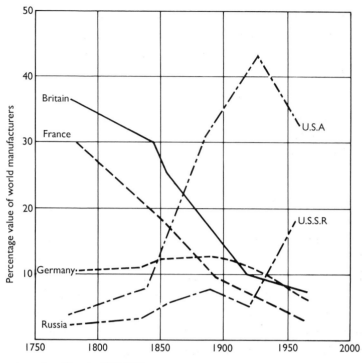

*Percentage of world trade, 1750-1960*

at safeguarding uncompetitive British manufactures. The free trade principles of John Bright and Richard Cobden of the Manchester School of political economists had played a major role in the development of nineteenth-century Liberalism. However, by the 1890s the Conservatives and a number of Liberals had begun to follow Chamberlain's lead in suggesting that Britain's perceived industrial decline had made protection a national economic necessity. 'Free Trade versus Tariff Reform' became a great economic and political debate in pre-1914 Britain.

## THE CRISIS IN INDUSTRIAL RELATIONS

The last quarter of the nineteenth century witnessed a rapid growth in the number of mass-membership trade unions, composed largely of unskilled or semi-skilled workers. This had taken place notably among such groups as the dockers, the transport workers, and the miners. These 'new' unions were eager to use their collective strength in a campaign for better wages and conditons. By 1890, they had already won some major victories; the gas workers had successfully struck for an eight-hour day, and the 'dockers' tanner' (sixpence a day basic pay rate) had been reluctantly granted by the port authorities.

The employers attempted to counter what they saw as a major threat to their interests by forming employers' federations, determined to resist the strength of organised labour. The scene was set for major conflict on the industrial front. Questions pressed themselves on the Government and on Parliament: what should their attitude be towards the struggle? At what point, if any, should the parties become involved in industrial relations and whose side should they take? The questions were particularly difficult ones for the Liberals. Those among them who still clung to Gladstonian principles of limited government action were reluctant to interfere in matters which they regarded as the province only of those directly concerned, the employers and their workers. In contrast, the more progressive Liberals argued that such matters were precisely those with which the party should be concerning itself. Indeed, it should be seeking to win the working classes to its side by taking up the cause of better working and living conditions. These polarised attitudes were a clear indication of the difficulties facing the Liberal Party in a changing Britain.

## THE QUESTION OF THE FRANCHISE

At the beginning of the twentieth century, Britain was not yet a democracy. Nevertheless, significant steps had been taken since 1832 to extend the franchise. By 1900, some 60 per cent of adult males had the vote. The question now arose: should the nation become fully democratised? This would involve, not only granting full adult male suffrage, but also, far more controversially, the enfranchising of women, the other half of the population. The battle over this became a dramatic feature of pre-1914 politics. It was an issue, moreover, which caused considerable dissension within the ranks of the Liberals, between those who saw universal suffrage as a logical and welcome constitutional progression and those who feared that such a huge increase in the electorate would introduce an unknown factor into British politics that might well have an irreversibly damaging effect on the Party's fortunes.

## THE POSITION OF THE HOUSE OF LORDS

The issue of democracy lay at the heart of another of the major controversies of the time. The two-chamber structure of the British Parliament meant that the House of Lords was constitutionally able to block the legislation sent up to it by the House of Commons. In practice, it was only measures presented by Liberal governments that the Lords chose to reject. This was because Conservative peers were in an overwhelming majority in the Upper House, which enabled the Conservative Party to wreck Liberal measures of which it disapproved. This occurred most strikingly in 1894 when Gladstone's Irish Home Rule Bill, having passed through the Commons, was then thrown out by the Lords. As Britain moved towards democracy, the question was how much longer the anomaly of an unelected assembly having an absolute veto over the elected chamber would be tolerated.

## THE ULSTER QUESTION

The Lords' behaviour over Home Rule was one aspect of the dominant and explosive issue of Ireland. Throughout the nineteenth century, Irish nationalists had been engaged in a desperate struggle to obtain the repeal of the 1801 Act of Union which had, against the wishes of the majority of the Irish people, incorporated the island of Ireland into the United Kingdom. Home Rule for Ireland was one obvious solution, but it met two major obstacles. One was the fear on the part of most Conservatives, and a good number of Liberals, that the loss of Ireland would be an unacceptable blow to both the unity of the United Kingdom and to the notion of Britain as an empire. The other was the position of Ulster. For historical reasons, which dated back to the enforced Elizabethan and Cromwellian land settlements, the northern Irish province of Ulster was peopled predominantly by Protestants of English and Scottish origin. They rejected any suggestion that the whole of Ireland should be separated from Britain, since this would, in their eyes, lead to the inevitable subjection of their province to the rule of an oppressive Catholic majority. The fears of Protestant Ulster were expressed in the simple couplet, 'Home Rule means Rome rule'. The Ulster question defied settlement and created a major divide in British politics. That the term Unionist was more commonly used at this time to describe the Conservative Party is one indication of how important the Irish issue was to contemporaries.

## BRITAIN'S ROLE AS AN EMPIRE

In the 30 years before the turn of the century Britain had vastly and rapidly increased the size of her existing empire. This was largely the result of her participation in the European scramble for Africa, which had begun in the 1870s. The major European colonial powers, France, Germany, Belgium and Britain laid claim to large areas of the African continent. No single motive explains their actions, but certainly thoughts of economic advantage and national pride helped to initiate the grab for African territory. The Conservatives under Disraeli had been particularly associated with this new phase of imperialism, but there were also Liberals, such as Joseph Chamberlain, who supported imperial expansion. By the end of the century there was considerable dispute between and within the parties as to whether Britain should continue to pursue expansionist policies or whether the traditional view, espoused earlier by such great Liberal figures as Bright and Gladstone, that imperialism was both immoral and a threat to international peace, should prevail. The two opposed viewpoints were to be bitterly and violently expressed at the time of the Anglo-Boer War (1899-1902).

## BRITAIN AND EUROPE

Closely associated with the issue of imperialism was the question of Britain's relations with Europe. For most of the nineteenth century Britain had tried to remain aloof from involvement in European affairs. This policy of detachment made sense so long as Britain saw herself as economically self-sufficient and militarily powerful. However, by the end of the century, she had become aware that she was no longer the leading industrial nation and that her naval strength, traditionally regarded as her strongest guarantee of security, was now being seriously challenged by the growth of Germany's war fleets. Such realisations led many politicians to urge that Britain should abandon her isolationism and seek defensive alliances and military agreements with friendly European powers.

The dilemma facing Britain in the early years of the new century was the degree to which she would commit herself to the alliance system that had begun to split Europe into two distinct camps, and with which of the sides she would ally herself. As European tension increased, the Liberals in particular were faced with making choices in foreign policy that were to have momentous consequences in 1914.

The issues discussed in this chapter represent the major concerns that shaped British politics in Lloyd George's time. They posed a set of questions which obliged the Liberal Party to re-examine its traditional values. How far was it willing to adjust itself to meet the pressures of the time? The Liberal Party held power in its own right from 1905 to 1915. It then continued, first with Asquith and then Lloyd George, to provide the Prime Minister for the series of coalition governments that operated until 1922. This gave the party a 17 year period of dominance in British politics, after which it was never again to hold office. At face value this would suggest that the period of Liberal rule had been a political failure. How far this was true and how it is to be explained are questions which continue to stimulate debate among historians.

*Points to consider*

1) How did the Liberal Party respond to the problem of poverty in Victorian England?
2) Distinguish between the principles of Free Trade and Protection.
3) What connection was there between the Ulster question and the House of Lords issue?
4) In this period, what political difficulties stood in the way of an extension of democracy?
5) Examine the problems attached to Britain's role as an imperial and European power.

# LLOYD GEORGE
# AND THE HISTORIANS

Lloyd George was not always an easy man to understand. Although he remained a Liberal throughout his career, the party label never adequately defined his attitude. Contemporaries found it difficult to detect precisely what his political motivations were; the economist, J.M. Keynes, went so far as to say that Lloyd George was 'rooted in nothing', meaning that he had no consistent principles but merely reacted to events as they occurred. Later commentators have continued to find him equally difficult to pin down. A.J.P. Taylor makes essentially the same point as Keynes:

> He cared nothing for the conventional rules – neither the rules of personal behaviour nor those economic rules of free enterprise to which his Liberal colleagues attached so much importance. Lloyd George lived in the moment, a master of improvisation.

Doubtless, there will never be complete agreement among historians and biographers about Lloyd George. Each new generation sees him through different eyes. About the facts of his career there is now little dispute. The publication of the greater part of his private correspondence and papers and the release of official documents have filled in most of the gaps. The differences are over interpretation. Was he a creative or a destructive force in British politics? What impact did he have on the Liberal Party? Did he pursue a consistent line of policy or was he simply an opportunist? These are the questions that tend to receive varying answers depending on the historical perception of the questioner.

There are literally hundreds of books dealing with Lloyd George and his times. The following list is not meant to be exhaustive and is certainly not inclusive of all the important works that have been published about him. But the hope is that it will point the reader towards some of the major studies of the subject.

Perhaps the best starting point is a work published in 1954, Frank Owen's, *Tempestuous Journey*. This is sympathetic to Lloyd George and represents the traditional view of him as the Welsh Nonconformist successfully making his way in a hostile political world by force of personality and dedication to radical principles. This helps to balance the view expressed in the 1930s by his political critics and opponents, such as J.M. Keynes, Stanley Baldwin and Ramsay MacDonald, that he was an unprincipled, destructive, power-seeker. J.M. Keynes, an influential Liberal who came to disapprove of Lloyd George, referred to him as 'the goat', a disparaging reference to his philandering in his private life as well as to his lack of political reliability. It was rumoured that Baldwin, the Conservative leader, so disliked Lloyd George that he took malicious pleasure in defacing photos of him when he came across them in books and newspapers. It was also said that Ramsay MacDonald, the Labour leader, visibly shuddered at the very name of Lloyd George.

The biographies written since his death in 1945, though more detached, have continued to divide broadly between those which treat him as a far-sighted political innovator and those which regard him as a powerful but ultimately unsuccessful political outsider. In simple terms, it could be said that Lloyd George is seen either as a winner or a loser, a creator or a destroyer. One of the outstanding modern biographies is John Grigg's detailed study, which first appeared in 1973, in which Grigg argues that far from being a Welsh outsider Lloyd George established himself as a constructive statesman in the mainsteam of British politics. Grigg makes due allowance for the many apparently contradictory features of Lloyd George's career. He suggests that the evident deviousness of much of Lloyd George's behaviour was no more than that necessarily engaged in by any politician who wants to get things done; the subtleties of the British political system do not allow for a consistently straightforward approach. Grigg believes that 'Lloyd George was both a crusader and a crook, but the crusader took precedence'. In saying this, Grigg is offering an answer to the basic question which concerns all historians who seek to understand Lloyd George's motivation. Robert Blake put the question in the following form; 'Was he a man of principle pursuing by devious means a consistent end, or was he an opportunist who relied upon his intuition to gratify at every turn his love of power and office?'

Another of the important biographies to appear in the 1970s was Peter Rowland's *Lloyd George*. While acknowledging his subject's great dynamism and flair, Rowland takes a generally unsympathetic view of him as a person and suggests that although his achievements were superficially impressive most of them lacked substance and permanence. Another critical, though at the same time very lively, analysis was provided in 1976 by Donald McCormick, the title of whose book neatly expressed its main thrust, *The Mask of Merlin*. This was a play on the contemporary description of Lloyd George as 'the Welsh wizard'. McCormick extended the metaphor by suggesting that Lloyd George was concerned with nothing higher than the advancement of his own career, which he achieved by using his personal magnetism to cast a series of political spells over his contemporaries.

A far more balanced interpretation has been offered by Kenneth Morgan, arguably the leading authority on Lloyd George and his times. In a series of major studies, he has reaffirmed the significance of Lloyd George by suggesting that he was 'the decisive catalyst in the transition from Victorian Britain to the new society of the twentieth century'. Morgan's claim rests on what he regards as Lloyd George's three principal achievements. More than any other single person Lloyd George was responsible for laying the foundations of the welfare state. Equally important, his career 'symbolised a new social revolution, that "the day of the cottage-bred man" had indeed dawned even in the stratified society of Edwardian Britain'. Morgan also emphasises Lloyd George's contribution as a Welshman to the growth of 'provincialism', the reaction of Wales, Scotland and northern England against what they perceived as their political and economic subordination to the interests of southern England.

Kenneth Morgan is one of the contributors to a major reappraisal of Lloyd George, published in 1991 as *The Life and Times of David Lloyd George* (edited by Judith Loades). Another outstanding scholar who contributed to that work was Martin Pugh. In his article, Pugh develops some of the ideas that he previously stated in his book, *Lloyd George*, an important recent study, drawing on many of the latest ideas and findings.

In Pugh's judgement, Lloyd George was not as a Welsh outsider, but a skilled operator who manoeuvred his way into the British political system and made it work for him for the greater part of his career. Influenced more by Joseph Chamberlain's ideas of state intervention than by traditional Liberalism, Lloyd George's radicalism was always broad enough to include the progressive elements in both Conservative and Labour politics. This breadth of approach made him appear lacking in fixed principles and meant that he did not belong comfortably in any of the parties. Hence, ultimately, despite his extraordinary achievements as a minister for eleven years and as a Prime Minister for six, his attempts to advance the cause of coalition or consensus politics succeeded in hastening the decline of the Liberal Party and reducing him to political impotence for the last 20 years of his life.

It is against this background of the decline of the Liberal Party that Lloyd George's career has to be set. For some 60 years now there has been a continuing debate among historians over the reasons for this decline. It is a crucial and directly relevant topic because it relates to the whole question of the character and structure of British politics in the twentieth century.

In 1934 an imporant work appeared which set the pattern for subsequent explanations of Liberal decline. In his expressively entitled book, *The Strange Death of Liberal England*, George Dangerfield argued that the great social, political and economic crises that afflicted Britain in the period before 1914 showed that the Liberal governments since 1905 had failed to meet the challenges of their time. The number and seriousness of the strikes called by aggressive trade unions, the riotous behaviour of suffragettes demanding votes for women, the bitter dispute between Lords and Commons over the reform of the House of Lords, Ulster on the brink of civil war over Home Rule: these conflicts were the evidence on which Dangerfield based his notion of Liberal failure. His argument was that the truculence of trade unions, suffragettes, peers, and Ulstermen indicated that by 1914 the Liberals had an outmoded political philosophy which inhibited them from adapting effectively to the pressures of the twentieth century. This explains the subsequent rapid decline of the Liberal Party, whose essential moderation could not cope with the pre-1914 unrest or with the demands placed upon the nation by the First World War.

Superficially, the extreme opposition to the Liberal governments does appear to indicate that their policies had failed to satisfy the major demands of the time. However, although Dangerfield's interpretation remains a provocative starting point, it has been largely superseded by another school of thought which stresses that, difficult though matters were for the Liberals, they were still in office in 1914 after nine years of unbroken government. All challenges to their authority had been contained. Contentious measures of the likes of the People's Budget, National Insurance, the Parliament Act and Home Rule had been forced through Parliament. Asquith's Cabinets had remained united throughout the troubles; no minister resigned office before 1914. Despite the great Liberal gains of the 1906 landslide victory being lost in the elections of 1910, the Unionists had not been able to oust Asquith's Government; although the Conservatives made electoral gains in the south of the country, the Liberals maintained their traditional support in the industrial and working class regions. Paul Adelman remarks: 'The Liberal Party may have been losing ground to the right, but it was warding off the challenge from the left'.

It is the resurgence of the Liberal Party in this period rather than its decline that has been strongly emphasised by Peter Clarke and Ross McKibbin. It is true that the Labour Party had grown in membership in the country at large, mainly through trade-union affiliation, but as a parliamentary force before 1914 it had, on its own admission, proved self-doubting and ineffectual, never remotely suggesting that it was capable of becoming a radical alternative government to the Liberals. Clarke suggests that the Labour Party had begun to see its future role not so much as a separate radical force but as part of a Liberal-Labour 'Progressive' movement.

All this tends to indicate that the problems of pre-1914 Britain were not a proof of the failure of Liberal policies since 1905. The decline of the Liberals as a political party may well owe more to the impact of the Great War and the political realignment that it caused. If this were so, then the demise of the Liberal Party was no more inevitable than was the rise of the Labour Party.

The role of the Labour Party has become a crucial part of the historiographical argument over Liberal decline. Until fairly recently there was a general assumption that given the changing nature of Britain in the early twentieth century, with an expanding and politically conscious working class in possession of the vote, the Labour Party was bound to take over from the Liberals as the voice of the workers. There was the further assumption that as politics became increasingly a struggle between the forces of capital and those of labour, the party whose very name made it the political representative of labour was destined to hold power. These assumptions are often referred to as 'the inevitability thesis', which may be understood as the idea that certain developments are predetermined and therefore certain to occur in the course of history. Martin Pugh defines it in these terms:

Up to the 1960s the field was held by a generation of historians and political scientists who had emerged in the post-1945 era when politics was dominated by the two parties [Conservative and Labour], one representing 'capital' and the other representing 'labour'. From this perspective the rise of the Labour Party appeared inevitable; after 1900 as the working class expanded its industrial and political organisation, the Liberals found themselves increasingly ground between the upper millstone of bourgeois Gladstonianism and the nether millstone of proletarian pressure for reform and power.

In analysing the past, historians are of course greatly affected by their own times. The challenge to historical determinism represented by the recent wholesale retreat from Marxism, following the collapse in the late 1980s and early 1990s of the Communist regimes in the USSR and the Eastern bloc, has made writers very wary of regarding any movement as inevitable. This is a point stressed by a number of modern writers. Peter Clarke observes that historians, who until recently approached the subject of Liberal decline from a 'sub-Marxian perspective', which led them to see the rise of Labour at the expense of the Liberals as an unavoidable part of the development of class politics, have now begun to doubt that interpretation. David Marquand has suggested that the general loss of confidence in Marxist analysis has encouraged scholars to appreciate that social and economic issues are too complex to be explained simply in terms of class conflict between the forces of capital and labour. Explanations of change which rely upon the notion of 'winners and losers' in history are held to be too determinist to be acceptable.

Furthermore, Marquand and another modern analyst, Duncan Tanner, have in separate studies pointed out that the historical strength of the Labour Party has been exaggerated. At no time in its 90 year history has it been able to win more than 48 per cent of the popular vote. Far from sharing office on a regular basis, according to the swing of the electoral pendulum, Labour has been in power for only 20 of the 70 years since it became the official opposition. Tanner also emphasises that the Labour Party was not so much a new socialist party as an offshoot of nineteenth-century radicalism. The reason why it took over from the Liberal Party had more to do with the oddities of the British electoral system than a straight rejection of Liberalism and a popular embracing of Labour.

The weighting to be given to the Labour Party as a cause of Liberal decline is one central historiographical problem. Another is how much significance to attach to the impact on Liberal fortunes of the 1914-18 war. In a celebrated study, published in 1966, Trevor Wilson suggested that the four years of total war from 1914 effectively ruined the Liberal Party by damaging its morale and creating a crisis of leadership. His main contention was that the restrictive measures resorted to by the State took the heart out of the Liberals by destroying their traditional beliefs in individual liberty. More seriously still, the formation of Lloyd George's Lib-Lab-Conservative coalition in 1916 divided the Liberal Party into two opposed sections, Lloyd George supporters and Asquithians, a division that could not be subsequently repaired. The results were seen in 1918 when, in the first election for eight years, the Conservative Coalitionists won an overwhelming victory. Asquith's Liberals were reduced to only 28 seats, less than half the number gained by the Labour Party. It is true that Lloyd George continued as Prime Minister, but his Liberal supporters had retained their seats only because the Conservatives had agreed not to put up rival candidates in their constituencies.

Wilson later said that his analysis had been pushed too far by some of his readers. He had not meant to imply that the war and the leadership question were the only causes of Liberal decline; he accepted that other longer-term factors may also have applied. Among these factors were the structural and constitutional changes that took place independently of the war.

A believer in the importance of the long-term causes of decline is Henry Pelling, an eminent scholar in the field of labour history. He suggests that while the Labour Party had not done well in pre-war elections, the increasing urbanisation of Britain and the huge increase both in trade-union membership and trade-union affiliations to the party gave it a financial and electoral potential that the Liberals could not match. That potential began to be tapped in 1918 as a result of a major constitutional change. In that year the Representation of the People Act increased the electorate from 7 million to 21 million, thereby establishing the mass electorate on which Labour was subsequently to draw.

*Points to consider*

1) Identify the differing views of Lloyd George as they have developed among major historians since 1954.
2) Define the main argument in George Dangerfield's, *The Strange Death of Liberal England*?
3) In assessing the reasons for the decline of the Liberal Party, what importance have historians attached to a) the rise of the Labour Party, and b) the impact of the 1914-18 War?

# 4

# LLOYD GEORGE'S EARLY CAREER

## THE POLITICAL SCENE, 1890-1906

Lloyd George entered a House of Commons in 1890 that was dominated by the Conservatives, as shown in the table below:

**TABLE 2**

| 1886 Election Result | Seats |
|---|---|
| Conservatives | 317 |
| Liberal Unionists | 77 |
| Liberals | 191 |
| Irish Nationalists | 85 |
| Total | 670 |

The Conservative dominance had begun in 1886 when the Liberals had split over Gladstone's introduction of the Irish Home Rule Bill, and continued, with the exception of a three-year period (1892-95), until 1905. Profound disagreement over Ireland was the key factor in the inability of the Liberals to mount a serious challenge to the Conservative Government in the 20 years after 1886. Those Liberals who broke away from Gladstone over Ireland became known as Liberal Unionists; by the end of the century they had permanently fused with the Conservatives, though they kept their separate name until 1912.

In 1890, the Irish Nationalists underwent a crisis when their leader, Parnell, was cited as a correspondent in a divorce case. The majority of the Catholic Irish felt that this disqualified him as their leader. Equally significantly in England, the Nonconformists, an influential religious grouping that traditionally supported the Liberal Party and which had been broadly sympathetic towards Home Rule, informed Gladstone that Parnell was no longer acceptable. Parnell died shortly after in 1891, but Gladstone believed that the impact of Parnell's fall from grace had effectively destroyed the chances of Home Rule being accepted by Parliament. Nevertheless, despite both his own misgivings and Chamberlain's informing him in 1891 that there was no chance of the Liberal Unionists returning to the Liberal fold, Gladstone persevered. Under him, the Liberal Party put forward its 'Newcastle Programme' in 1891, advocating Home Rule, as well as disestablishment of the Anglican Church in Wales, land reform, recognition of the liability of employers for industrial injuries, and further extension of the franchise. The results of the election that Salisbury called in 1892 suggested that the Liberals had made at least a partial recovery:

## TABLE 3

| 1892 Election Result | Seats |
|---|---|
| Conservatives | 268 |
| Liberal Unionists | 46 |
| Liberals | 272 |
| Irish Nationalists | 80 |
| Others | 4 |
| Total | 670 |

With the backing of the Irish Nationalists, Gladstone was again able to form a government. In 1893 he introduced his second Home Rule Bill, which was accepted by the Commons but rejected by the Lords. Gladstone resigned soon after and announced his retirement from politics. In his last parliamentary speech he warned prophetically that a final struggle between Lords and Commons could not be long avoided. His place as leader and Prime Minister was taken in 1894 by Lord Rosebery. Once Gladstone had gone, Joseph Chamberlain became the major figure in British politics. The young Lloyd George was greatly impressed by him.

Rosebery's Government did not last long. The lack of an overall

Liberal majority and the Conservative domination of the House of Lords prevented any measures of note being introduced and passed. Rosebery resigned in June 1895 after a defeat in the Commons; Conservative government was then renewed under Lord Salisbury. Significantly, Salisbury's new Cabinet included two prominent former Liberals, Lord Hartington, who had represented the old-style Whig element in the Liberal Party, and Joseph Chamberlain. These appointments reflected the seriousness of the division among the Liberals now that Gladstone's personal leadership was no longer there to hold them together. This division was a factor in their heavy defeat in the ensuing election.

## TABLE 4

| 1895 Election Result | Seats |
|---|---|
| Conservatives | 340 |
| Liberal Unionists | 71 |
| Liberals | 177 |
| Irish Nationalists | 82 |
| Total | 670 |

The presence of Chamberlain in the Government raised expectations that the Conservatives might move towards social reform, and it is true that they introduced a Workmen's Compensation Act in 1897, and discussed the feasibility of old age pensions. But Chamberlain's post was that of Colonial Secretary and it was imperial issues that dominated politics in this period, pushing domestic reform into the background.

There was no single attitude among Liberals towards imperialism. Many Liberals supported the idea of imperial expansion. Rosebery (Prime Minister 1894-95 and Liberal leader 1894-96), Herbert Asquith (Prime Minister after 1908), and Edward Grey (Foreign Secretary after 1905) were prominent among the Liberal Imperialists.

Notable among those who opposed expansion were Herbert Gladstone (Liberal Chief Whip, 1899-1905) and John Morley (Secretary for India 1905-10), representing what was often referred to as the 'Little Englander' attitude, an approach associated with W.E. Gladstone and the Liberal anti-imperial tradition. Lloyd George gravitated towards the latter group. His interest and that of the nation at large in imperial affairs was quickened by Britain's involvement in Africa. Tension with France over rival colonial claims in north Africa almost led to war in 1898, the same year which saw the reassertion of British authority in the Sudan following Kitchener's victory at Omdurman. But it was southern Africa that became the vital area around which the debate within Britain over imperialism was concentrated.

By the 1880s, southern Africa had been divided between the Dutch Boers (farmers), occupying the Transvaal and the Orange Free State, and the British, settled in the Cape Province. Friction between the two types of settlers was constant. In 1881, Gladstone's Government had recognised Boer rights of self-government in the Transvaal but ambiguously had still claimed British 'suzerainty' in the region. Following the discovery of extensive gold fields there in 1886, the Boers under their President, Paul Kruger, feared that their young and underpopulated country would be swamped by the prospectors and traders, who had flooded in hoping for rich pickings. The ill-disciplined ways of these *Uitlanders* (Afrikaans for foreigners), who were largely of British and German stock, were wholly alien to the sober, God-fearing, Boers. Determined to preserve their cultural identity from foreign pollution, the Boers refused to extend political or electoral rights to these obnoxious newcomers.

This provided the pretext for Chamberlain to interfere. From the Colonial Office, he demanded that the principle of equal constitutional rights for all inhabitants of the Transvaal be applied. The Boers stoutly refused, as Chamberlain had hoped they would. There is now little doubt that Chamberlain was spoiling for a fight. In 1895, he had been deeply implicated in the Jameson Raid, an abortive attempt to topple Kruger's government by organising a rising of the *Uitlanders*. Chamberlain's secret correspondence with Alfred Milner, whom he appointed in 1897 as the High Commissioner in the Cape, shows beyond doubt that his deliberate aim was to manoeuvre the Boers into a position where they had no recourse but to fight. Indeed, Chamberlain had selected Milner knowing well that the Commissioner's temperament and total belief in the supremacy of British claims in Southern Africa would make the breakdown of negotiations with the Boers unavoidable. This duly happened in 1899, when Kruger, exasperated by Britain's demands as expressed by Milner, abandoned any further talks. In October, the two Boer republics declared war on Britain, a war that was to last for three years.

Suggestions that the Anglo-Boer conflict was 'Milner's War' or 'Joe's War' stress the significance of the personalities of the leading figures in the drama. This is not to deny that deeper questions were involved. The outstanding issue was who was to run South Africa. Was it to be a British-dominated federal dominion or a Boer republic? For imperialists at home, both Conservative and Liberal, the first proposition was the only acceptable answer.

However, from the beginning there was a significant group in Britain who were deeply unhappy with the war. Referred to as 'pro-Boers', they questioned the moral validity of Britain's stance. Strength was given to their case by the failure of British forces to win the war quickly, a failure which brought Britain considerable international embarrassment. Still more discomforting to the Government were the reports of the extreme measures which the British forces employed in order to break Boer resistance. The most notorious of these was the internment of civilians in 'concentration' camps, where the cramped and unhygienic conditions frequently led to the spread of fatal diseases. Henry Campbell-Bannerman, who had become Liberal leader in 1899, accused Salisbury's government of employing 'the methods of barbarism'. Lloyd George declared: 'we have now taken to killing babies'.

Initially, however, the war had proved widely popular in Britain, and Prime Minister Salisbury sought to gain from this by calling an election in 1900. The Conservatives deliberately played the patriotic card in what became known as the 'Khaki election'.

Although the Conservative majority was slightly reduced, the Government still had a comfortable lead. Six years later, however, it suffered a landslide defeat at the hands of the Liberals, who were left with a majority over the Conservatives of 243.

The remarkable recovery of the Liberals in 1906 after 20 years in the doldrums was only marginally the result of their own efforts. There is a maxim: oppositions do not win elections, governments lose them. This can certainly be applied to the Liberal victory of 1906, which was largely due to the mistakes and failures of the Conservatives since 1900. Arthur Balfour, who succeeded Salisbury as Prime Minister in July 1902 inherited a number of growing problems. By the time he took over, the

**TABLE 5**

| 1900 Election Result | Seats |
|---|---|
| Conservatives | 334 |
| Liberal Unionists | 68 |
| Liberals | 184 |
| Labour (LRC) | 2 |
| Irish Nationalists | 82 |
| Total | 670 |

Government's mishandling of the Boer War, which was not finally won by Britain until May 1902, had begun to cause a considerable loss of popularity. To this could be added a long list of political liabilities.

The Government was tainted by its association with 'Chinese slavery' in southern Africa, the charge being that it had permitted large numbers of coolies to be brought from Asia to work in the diamond and gold mines in appalling conditions for pitiful wages. Further trouble for the Conservatives followed the introduction in 1902 of Balfour's Education Bill. In most respects this was a highly progressive measure, but since it abolished the old school boards and placed responsibility for educational provision in the hands of the local authorities, it aroused the bitter opposition of the Nonconformists who complained that now that education was to be paid for out of the rates, Anglican schools would, in effect, be publicly subsidised. The pro-Liberal 'Nonconformist conscience', which throughout the nineteenth century had played a major part in the formation of public attitudes on moral issues, had also expressed itself in the loud objections of the temperance lobby to the clause in the Government's Licensing Act of 1904, which provided compensation for landlords and brewers who were to lose their licences under the new regulations governing the liquor industry.

The problem for any government seeking to introduce reform is that it is bound to upset vested interests. This had shown itself in 1902 when George Wyndham, the Secretary for Ireland, had introduced his Land Bill, providing tenants with £100 million to buy out their landlords. Although the measure effectively ended the land problem in Ireland, it received scant praise from the Irish nationalists who merely regarded it as long overdue, while the Unionists looked askance at an act that to them represented a bowing before nationalist pressure.

Further harm to the Government's reputation occurred as a result of the Taff Vale decision of 1901. In 1900, the Taff Vale Railway Company in South Wales sued the railway union, the ASRS, for damages resulting from a strike. A series of contradicatory findings in the lower courts led to a hearing in the House of Lords, sitting as the final Court of Appeal; the Lords ruled against the ASRS. This decision reinforced the belief among trade unionists that British law was fundamentally inimical to their interests. With the Conservative Government resolute against legislating to reverse the Taff Vale decision, and the Liberals impotent in opposition, the argument for a separate political party to represent the unions' cause became irresistible to the leaders of organised labour. By 1903, 127 unions had affiliated to the Labour Representation Committee. Direct working-class involvement in parliamentary politics was now a reality.

The effect of these various issues and measures was to undermine the strength of the Conservative Government and make it electorally vulnerable. Above all, it was the issue of tariff reform that weakened the Conservatives. In 1903, in an ill-advised attempt to outflank the opposition on economic matters, the government allowed itself to be persuaded to adopt Joseph Chamberlain's protectionist imperial preference policies as its official programme.

Few Conservatives fully understood tariff reform as a policy; they embraced it because it seemed to offer them a way of raising national income without resorting to taxation. Their uncertainty left them open to counter-attacks from the Liberals, who gratefully seized the opportunity to present themselves as the defenders of cheap and plentiful food against the 'hunger-mongering' advocates of tariff reform. A major and acrimonious campaign divided the nation. The Liberals with their 'big loaf' of free trade, symbolising cheap and plentiful food, versus the 'little loaf' of tariff reform, symbolising high prices and shortages, were judged by the electorate to have won the argument. Imperial preference was very much a one-man policy. Joseph Chamberlain always made an impact when he appeared personally. But apart from him, few tariff reformers were able to put across a convincing message or carry a successful campaign. The Liberals reaped the reward in 1906, when Campbell-Bannerman, who had become Prime Minister of a minority Liberal government in December 1905 following Balfour's resignation, led his party to a resounding victory. In the words of a contemporary,

*A Liberal poster of 1906*

'the Conservatives in 1906 went into the polling-booths with the albatross of tariff reform about their necks'.

## LLOYD GEORGE'S RISE TO POLITICAL PROMINENCE

In his biography of Lloyd George, Martin Pugh writes in an early chapter of his subject's 'escaping from Wales'. This is an apt way of referring to the nature of Lloyd George's political rise. Not unnaturally, his first concerns were Welsh, but his long-term objectives were national. Since Wales was Lloyd George's home base there is no surprise in his taking up Welsh causes. Nor is there any surprise in his moving on from those to broader issues. This has sometimes been represented as if it were a betrayal of his political roots, but every politician has to start somewhere. Stephen Constantine, in an essay published in 1992, writes memorably that Lloyd George's being born in 1863 was 'a shrewd career move', the suggestion being that in entering public life at a critical time in the reformation of British politics, he was in a position to shape his career around the great issues of the day.

*Lloyd George, aged 16*

Although he tended for political purposes to exaggerate the humble-ness of his background there is no reason to doubt that his upbringing in rural Wales gave him a genuine sympathy for the underdog. His dislike of privilege, particularly of what he called 'landlordism', drew him towards the radical section of the Liberal Party. Throughout his career, Lloyd George maintained an interest in land reform; a particular example is his launching in 1912 of a 'Land Campaign' aimed at guaranteeing minimum wages for farm labourers and creating special land courts to protect the interests of the underprivileged in rural areas.

If his radicalism was characteristic, so too was his willingness to compromise in order to gain a subsequent advantage. Until the late 1880s, rank-and-file members were not represented in the National Liberal federations, the main organising bodies of the Liberal Party. Lloyd George had to tread carefully not to offend the susceptibilities of the established members of the party. From the first he showed a readiness to temper his radicalism with the necessary discretion. In his first campaign in 1890, in the Caernarvon Boroughs by-election, he was careful not to upset the largely landed electorate by appearing too openly radical too soon. He also toed the Gladstonian line by declaring his support for Irish Home Rule. His earlier years in Welsh local politics had taught him the benefits of being adaptable. Biographers have referred, for example, to his ability to deliver a powerful temperance lecture that delighted his teetotal Uncle Lloyd, while still being ready to drink in the convivial company of his legal colleagues. In one sense this is hypocrisy; a less critical view is that it shows both an awareness on his part that there is more than one side to a question and a desire to respect other people's sensibilities.

The Welsh MPs whom Lloyd George joined in 1890 were largely radical in outlook, but since as a group they did not pursue a policy of national separatism they were never the divisive or dramatic force in British politics that the Irish Home Rulers were. Welsh issues never aroused the same parliamentary excitement as Irish affairs. Lloyd George's recognition of the limited political prospects offered him by purely Welsh matters led him to regard them as subordinate to larger Liberal concerns. His mind had been sharpened on this matter by his failure in 1896 to persuade the Liberal constituencies in southern Wales to join those in the north in a broad national front. The other MPs considered he had gone behind their backs in an attempt to make himself

Welsh leader. It would be wrong in any case to suppose that he had a real chance of leading Wales politically. Southern Wales, the industrial and commercial region of the country, never fully accepted him. He was identified essentially with the Welsh-speaking north, which as a predominantly agricultural region was never in a position to take the leading role in the nation's affairs. This doubtless explains Lloyd George's rejection of the offer made to him in 1898 of the Chairmanship of the group of Welsh MPs at Westminster. Clearly, he visualised his public future as being in the mainsteam of British politics.

Although it was not until the end of his first decade as an MP that Lloyd George made a major contribution to the larger Liberal concerns, he had followed them with profound interest. His correspondence is revealing in this regard. As a young politician in the 1880s he had come privately to regard Gladstone's official Liberal policy as out of date. He had been attracted by Chamberlain's Unauthorised Programme with its emphasis on taxation and land duties. He considered the Liberal electoral successes in 1885 as owing more to support for Chamberlain than for Gladstone. Similarly, he viewed the Liberal victory in 1892 as more the result of the lack-lustre campaign of the Conservatives than to the attraction of such manoeuvres as Gladstone's Newcastle Programme of 1891, which he saw as a belated and rather desperate attempt to appease the radicals.

When Chamberlain broke away from Gladstone and the Liberals, Lloyd George's political affections turned towards Lord Rosebery. Now that his former hero had defected to the Unionists, Lloyd George looked upon Rosebery as the most progressive force in Liberalism. Even after Rosebery resigned from the Liberal Party leadership in 1896, Lloyd George continued to regard him as the individual most likely to unite the party while in opposition. What he found attractive was Rosebery's commitment to social reform and his firm defence of Britain's overseas interests. This latter point may seem a strange one in view of Lloyd George's pro-Boer stance over the war in southern Africa, the issue which in 1899 brought him to national prominence. It is important to understand his attitude; Lloyd George was certainly not an out-and-out imperialist, but neither was he a pacifist. He was not against war in principle. He opposed Britain's involvement in the south African war, because he regarded it as unnecessary:

There may be something to be said for a war so long as it is entered upon for an unselfish purpose. The influence of a war must always be brutalising, at best; but still if you enter upon it for an unselfish purpose, there is something which almost consecrates the sacrifices, bloodshed, and suffering endured. But when you enter upon a war purely and simply for the purposes of plunder, I know of nothing which is more degrading to the country or more hideous in its effects on the mind and character of the people engaged in it.

He believed that Britain could extend her legitimate interests in southern Africa without recourse to war. In attacking the Government he made much of the cost of the war; here was money, he argued, that would have been better spent on social welfare. The Boer War had thus provided him with an ideal opportunity to impress himself upon the nation at large. He took a high moral tone, condemning the war as an unjustifiable act of aggression and a waste of precious resources. His impact as an opponent of the war matched that of Chamberlain as a proponent. The vehemence Lloyd George aroused was evident in a notorious incident in December 1901 when he narrowly escaped serious physical injury after being prevented by a mob from giving a speech in Birmingham, Chamberlain's stronghold; fearing for his life, the police smuggled him out of the hall disguised as one of themselves.

Throughout his campaign against the war, Lloyd George tried not to antagonise the Liberal Imperialists. In particular, he was at pains not to distance himself from Rosebery. It was to him rather than to Campbell-Bannerman, the official party leader, that Lloyd George still looked as the figure best able to reunite the Liberals. A strong element of self-interest was also involved; at a critical juncture in his career Lloyd George was anxious not to close any avenues of possible advancement within the party by becoming too closely associated with any one faction. He was not to know that Rosebery would soon lose interest and drift out of the political scene. But this in itself did Lloyd George no great harm; by then he had established himself as a conciliator within the Party.

His capacity for keeping things in balance, thereby obtaining the best of both worlds, was evident in his reaction to Balfour's Education Bill introduced in 1901. The outraged Nonconformists had mounted a campaign against the subsidising of Anglican schools from the rates.

Lloyd George's private judgement was that the church schools, particularly in Wales, needed such a Bill to improve their efficiency and quality, but he judged that the Nonconformists would expect their interests to be protected by the Liberals. Consequently he kept his own acceptance quiet and undertook to represent the Welsh Nonconformists. It was never his intention to stop the Bill, but he was successful in lessening Nonconformist anger by modifying the Bill in certain respects as it applied to Wales, such as the abandonment of religious tests for teachers.

Having inadvertently allowed the Liberals to come off best over the Boer War, the Conservative Government also permitted them to steal the advantage over protection. The culprit was again Chamberlain. In effect, he was trying to graft onto Conservatism an economic policy that was essentially a new form of radicalism. Richard Jebb, a leading tariff reformer of the time, later admitted as much. He described the adoption by the Conservatives of Chamberlain's schemes as having been fraudulent: 'We were running a radical policy, to suit our purpose, which was Liberal Unionist'. All this offered Lloyd George an easy target for his shafts of wit and ridicule. As to his own views, he did not start from a theoretical base. For obvious party political reasons he paid lip service to free trade as a principle, but his concern was a practical one. As he showed later when in office, Lloyd George was essentially concerned with administration, with getting things done. Moreover, his concept of free trade certainly did not exclude state intervention where necessary. His major contribution to the debate started by Chamberlain in 1903 was to mock the ambiguities of the term 'protection' and impose on the argument his own vision of social justice:

> There is abundant wealth in this country, and by its side there is hideous poverty. If the Cabinet want an inquiry, let them inquire into that. Mr. Chairman, I also am a protectionist. I avow myself a man who believes in protecting industry. Yes, I would protect people – not from honest labour abroad – I would protect the agricultural industry from the extortion that confiscates its improvements. I would protect the education of the sons and daughters of the people from the black sceptre of the priest. I would protect labour from unconscionable tyranny and oppression . . . . And above all I would protect indusry from that terrible evil

which is worse here than in any land, that ill which is enfeebling the health, the strength, the intelligence, which oppresses the people in their effort not merely in the struggle with foreign foes, but in that nobler struggle to rise up to a healthier, a purer and a nobler zone of life.

How far the Conservatives had lost the argument over protection was revealed in the 1906 election. Balfour, hoping that the disagreements in the Liberal Party would leave it incapable of governing effectively, resigned in December 1905, leaving Campbell-Bannerman to form an administration. Balfour's ruse did not work; in the 1906 election, the voters, more conscious of Conservative failures than of Liberal divisions, put the new government back into power with a handsome majority.

**TABLE 6**

| 1906 Election Result | Votes | Seats | % vote |
|---|---|---|---|
| Conservatives | 2 451 454 | 157 | 43.6 |
| Liberals | 2 757 883 | 400 | 49.0 |
| Labour | 329 748 | 30 | 5.9 |
| Irish Nationalists | 35 031 | 83 | 0.6 |

Electorate – 7 264 883     Turnout – 82.6%

The size of their majority seemed to guarantee the Liberals years of government. Lloyd George, who had already been rewarded for his contribution to the unseating of the Conservatives by being made President of the Board of Trade, now had the opportunity to put his radical ideas into practical effect.

| *timeline* | 1863 | Born in Manchester, on the 17 January |
|---|---|---|
| | 1864 | Moves to Llanystumdwy, North Wales   *(1)* |
| | 1864-77 | Brought up by his shoemaker uncle, Richard Lloyd   *(1-14)* |
| | 1878 | Starts work in a solicitor's office in Portmadoc   *(15)* |
| | 1880 | His first newspaper article published   *(17)* |
| | 1882-5 | Member of the Caernarvonshire Local Volunteers   *(19-22)* |

| | |
|---|---|
| 1884 | Passes law exam and enters legal practice in Wales *(21)* |
| 1886-7 | Secretary of local Anti-Tithe League *(23-24)* |
| 1888 | Marries Margaret Owen *(25)* |
| 1889 | Elected as local councillor in Caernarvon *(26)* |
| 1890 | Liberal MP for Caernarvon Borough *(27)* |
| 1891 | Attacks Conservative Education Bill *(28)* |
| 1892 | General Election – Liberal Government formed *(29)* |
| 1893-5 | Campaigns for Welsh Church Disestablishment *(30-32)* |
| 1898 | Forms Welsh National Liberal Council *(35)* |
| 1899-1902 | Attacks the Conservative Government's conduct of the Boer War *(36-39)* |
| 1902 | Attacks Balfour's Education Bill *(39)* |
| 1903-05 | Leads the Liberal offensive against Chamberlain's tariff reform programme *(40-42)* |
| 1905 | President of the Board of Trade *(42)* |

*(numbers in brackets refer to his age)*

## Points to consider

1) **Why were the Unionists in power for the greater part of the period, 1890-1906?**
2) **Why was Ireland such a dominant political issue in this period?**
3) **In what sense was the Anglo-Boer War (1899-1902) 'Joe's War'?**
4) **Account for the heavy defeat of the Unionists in the 1906 election.**
5) **Assess the importance to Lloyd George of Welsh affairs in this period.**
6) **What part did a) the Anglo-Boer War, and b) the tariff reform issue, play in Lloyd George's rise to national prominence?**

# LLOYD GEORGE AND THE LIBERAL REFORMS, 1906–11

The years 1906-14 proved to be one of the most remarkable reforming periods in British history. The social measures introduced by the Liberals, touching variously on education, liquor licensing, prisons, old age pensions, national insurance, minimum wages, anti-sweating regulations and labour exchanges were an extraordinary achievement. If to these social policies are added the reform of the House of Lords, a Home Rule Act for Ireland, and the disestablishment of the Welsh Church, the range of reform is unprecedentedly wide. Whether the social reforms made up an identifiable package and whether they were inspired by a single Liberal ideology is debatable, but there is little doubting the importance of these measures. New Liberalism, with its belief in the responsibility of the State to improve social conditions, seemed to have come into its own.

Campbell-Bannerman, the Liberal Prime Minister from 1905 to 1908, usually receives scant attention in the history books, but it should not be overlooked that it was he who gave the impetus to Liberal reform. He truly believed that the 1906 election had given the party a mandate to pursue radical policies. It was also Campbell-Bannerman who in 1907 proposed the end of the House of Lords' absolute veto, thereby taking the first step towards the undermining of the Lords four years later.

## LLOYD GEORGE AT THE BOARD OF TRADE AND AT THE EXCHEQUER

For Lloyd George, his two and a half years as President of the Board of

Trade enabled him to establish his credentials as an administrator. Before 1905 he had proved a highly effective political campaigner and critic; now he was able to build his reputation as a minister. For the next 17 years he was never to be out of ministerial office. He brought to his leadership of the various departments he headed a willingness to take advice and to involve the interested parties in the preparation of legislation. This readiness to consult, if not rely on, experts is of a piece with his later efforts on the broader political front to introduce the concept of consensus politics and coalition government. What should be stressed is the dynamism that Lloyd George brought to the task. He provided the energy that turned ideas into reality. It is not Lloyd George's creativity, but his drive and perseverance that commands the historian's attention.

By any measure, Lloyd George's first ministerial post proved a major success. The legislative record of the Board of Trade was outstanding and far surpassed any of the other departments in Campbell-Bannerman's Government. Among the many measures introduced under Lloyd George's enthusiastic direction were Acts concerning Merchant Shipping, the Census of Production, Companies Amendment, Patents and Designs, and the Port of London Authority. What was particularly remarkable about them was that each involved an extension of State direction in economic and social affairs. In particular, the Merchant Shipping Act laid down restrictions on foreign shipping that were, in effect, protectionist. It was evident from the first that, although the Liberal government would continue to espouse the cause of free trade, it was in practice ready to bend its own rules.

In 1908, Herbert Asquith became Prime Minister on the retirement of Campbell-Bannerman through ill-health. Asquith took the obvious step of appointing Lloyd George as Chancellor of the Exchequer. This was in part an acknowledgement of his achievement at the Board of Trade; it was also aimed at strengthening party unity. In a certain sense, Asquith and Lloyd George represented, respectively, the moderate and radical forces in the new Liberalism. Asquith, the patrician, appointed Lloyd George, the man of the people, with the aim of placating the radical faction of the Liberals. It would be wrong, however, to suggest that the two men held opposing views on any major issue. The idea that the Prime Minister had to hold his Chancellor in check in case he ran away on too radical a programme does not fit the record. Indeed, much of what Lloyd George introduced as Chancellor had already been prepared by Asquith while he was at the Exchequer. What was different about the two men was their style and personality, rather than their politics. While they were never close personally, they respected and admired each other's qualities. Their 11 years as cabinet colleagues between 1905 and 1916, collaborating on a range of controversial issues, showed how well they could work together. That they later came to represent two opposed factions within the Liberal Party should not be allowed to distort the record of their former relationship, which had always been co-operative and amicable.

It is striking how large a part the issue of tariff reform played in the politics of the period. Despite the Conservatives' election defeat over this issue in 1906 and the retirement from active politics of Joseph Chamberlain, incapacitated by a stroke in that same year, the protectionists continued to agitate vigorously. The Conservatives believed it was the issue best calculated to revive their own fortunes and discomfort the Government. By-election results which showed a swing towards tariff reform candidates gave substance to their belief. The defeat of Winston Churchill (who succeeded Lloyd George at the Board of Trade) in a by-election in 1908 was a striking example of what could happen. Although Churchill's rejection owed more to constituency problems than to tariff reform, and he soon re-entered the Commons by way of a safe seat, his original defeat was an unwelcome rebuff to the Government.

It was vital, therefore, for the Liberals to succeed as a reforming government, while at the same time preventing economic decline. The argument over free trade would be won or lost by their success or failure in this regard. This was why the arguments that divided the parties over the Liberal measures were largely concerned not with the detail of the reforms themselves but how they were to be financed.

## OLD AGE PENSIONS AND THE PEOPLE'S BUDGET, 1908-09

The introduction of old age pensions in 1908 is undoubtedly a landmark in welfare provision, yet it was not regarded as a particularly revolutionary measure at the time. State pensions had often been discussed by both parties during the previous 20 years; in 1899, Lloyd

George had been a member of a parliamentary committee that had examined the matter. A number of other countries had already introduced such pensions, and Lloyd George had visisted Germany to observe the particular scheme in operation there. It could be argued that the measure was overdue rather than a dramatic departure. The first pensions granted 5s (25p) a week to people over 70 years old with incomes of less than £31 10s (£31.50p) a year. Although it had been Asquith who had introduced old age pensions in his 1908 budget, it was Lloyd George who subsequently became responsible for steering them through Parliament and implementing them.

It was in order to fund old age pensions that Lloyd George drew up his 1909 budget, destined to become known because of its apparent bias against the propertied classes as 'the People's Budget'. It eased the tax burden on lower wage-earners, but raised the tax on higher earned and on all unearned incomes, and introduced a 'super tax' of 5d (approximately 2½p) in the pound on incomes in excess of £5,000 p.a. Most controversially of all, it proposed death duties on inherited property and a levy of 20 per cent on the profits made from land sales. It was this last proposal that aroused the bitter opposition of the landed interests who claimed that they were the victims of a form of class war started by Lloyd George. He accepted that it was indeed a war, but not of that kind:

> This is a War Budget. It is for raising money to wage implacable warfare against poverty and squalidness. I cannot help hoping and believing that before this generation has passed away we shall have advanced a great step towards that good time when poverty and wretchedness and human degradation which always follow in its camp will be as remote to the people of this country as the wolves which once infested its forests.

Politically, the People's Budget should be seen as an attempt to destroy protectionism, to prove that by reallocating existing financial resources the worst of poverty and deprivation could be overcome without recourse to the dangers of tariff reform.

Perhaps no single issue is as helpful to an understanding of new Liberalism as taxation. Lloyd George's tax reforms were based on the notion of the redistribution of income. This marked a major step forward. Previously taxation had been broadly thought of as a means of

## RICH FARE.

THE GIANT LLOYD-GORGIBUSTER: "FEE, FI, FO, FAT,
I SMELL THE BLOOD OF A PLUTOCRAT;
BE HE ALIVE OR BE HE DEAD,
I'LL GRIND HIS BONES TO MAKE MY BREAD."

raising State revenue to meet a particular need, such as war expenditure. The new form aimed to redistribute income by taking from those who could pay and redirecting it to alleviate the distress of those who could not. It ceased to be merely a matter of financial adjustment and became one of implementing social justice. This in itself was a challenge to the traditional Liberal notion of individual freedom. It was equivalent to the State's saying that it required its richer citizens to be responsible for the improvement of its poorer ones. This was why stress was laid on direct taxation, calculated by reference to the individual's ability to pay, rather than on indirect taxation, which was indiscriminate in its effect, since it was placed on commodities and took no account of the buyer's resources.

*Lloyd George's inscription on the first page of his People's Budget; 'to Uncle Lloyd the real author of this Budget with his pupil's affectionate gratitude, May 31st 1910'*

As with old age pensions, one should not attribute total originality to Lloyd George. Even before 1906, there had been an increasing willingness to consider redistributive taxation. Moderate Liberals, however, distinguished between earned and unearned income. The former was regarded as productive wealth, the latter as unproductive. To tax the first variety was not acceptable since it contravened the traditional free-market, *laissez-faire* principles of Liberalism. But to tax unproductive wealth was considered perfectly proper. Harcourt, the Chancellor of the Exchequer in Gladstone's last ministry in 1894, had contemplated using death duties as a means of taxing unearned income. Thus there were Liberal precedents for the proposals in the People's Budget to tax unearned wealth and land values by introducing super-tax, land tax and death duties, measures which would leave the majority of middle class incomes untouched and would not affect the earnings of the working class at all.

Lloyd George rejected the charge that these measures were socialist. They were intended to benefit the whole community by redistributing wealth and unlocking previously unused financial resources. He specifically denied that he was engaged in class warfare; he claimed to be appealing not simply to the working class, but to all classes, indeed to all persons who genuinely earned their incomes. He presented it as a matter of social equity. His hope was that by attacking the idle rich he would unite in support of his measures all those who worked for their living, the industrious middle class as well as the industrial workers.

It is interesting, and at first sight surprising, that welfare reform frequently encountered resistance from those groups in society who were intended to be the chief beneficiaries. Why this was so illustrates one of the basic difficulties for the Liberals. Many working-class people shared a long-standing suspicion towards State intervention. Their practical experience of such developments as the workhouse, compulsory education, slum clearance and vaccination had not always been a happy one and did not endear them to the prospect of further State interference in their lives. Such people needed convincing that the State could protect their interests better than they themselves could. Writing in 1912, R. H. Tawney, one of the outstanding social historians of his day and a strong Labour Party supporter, explained why the intended recipients of welfare reform were initially so suspicious:

> The middle and upper class view in social reform is that it should regulate the worker's *life* in order that he may *work* better. The working class view of economic reform is that it should regulate his *work*, in order that he may have a chance of living. Hence to working people licensing reform, insurance acts, etc. seems beginning at the wrong end.

Given this attitude, the argument about the acceptability of State welfare schemes tended to focus on the question whether they were contributory or not. Old age pensions, entitlement to which depended solely on the recipient's age, were obviously attractive since they did not involve contributions. In contrast, national insurance, introduced in 1911, was a matter of compulsory contributions.

## NATIONAL INSURANCE
—
# THE DAWN OF HOPE.

*1911 Liberal Party poster*

The National Insurance Act of 1911 provided cover against sickness and unemployment for workers aged between 16 and 70; it did not apply to all industries, but was targeted at those where unemployment was consistently high. It was to be financed by contributions from the State, the employer and the employee, which were obligatory and would be deducted at source. Understandably, therefore, the measure had a rough ride. Calculations indicate that by the beginning of the century some five and a half million people belonged to schemes run by the insurance companies, friendly societies and the trade unions. It took time to convince the workers that they were going to gain more from an imposed State plan than from insurance policies they had chosen to take out for themselves. The popular press attacked the compulsory contributions as theft from the workers' pay packets. Moreover, the insurance societies, fearful of losing business on a huge scale to the State schemes, were at first extremely hostile.

It was a measure of Lloyd George's political realism and of his skill as a negotiator that instead of trying to fight the insurance companies he successfully invited them to join him in operating the unemployment insurance schemes. He adopted the same approach towards the British Medical Association, which throughout the twentieth century has often been obstructive to health reforms. It was only when Lloyd George convinced the BMA that doctors would gain even higher incomes from working within the health insurance scheme that it agreed to co-operate.

Significantly, the Labour Party, while fully committed to the principle of national insurance, initially opposed Lloyd George's plan for compulsory contributions; their counter proposal took the form of social benefits funded from taxation. (Lloyd George eventually won them over by promising to introduce payment for MPs, a commitment which he duly honoured in 1911). There had also been resistance to Churchill's Trade Boards Act of 1909 which aimed at providing minimum wages in the notorious 'sweated' industries, where a surplus of workers made it easy for employers to recruit labour on the cheap. The immediate effect of a minimum wage was to dry up job opportunities, which hardly served the interests of the workers. The concept of the minimum wage was also seen as cutting across the customary freedom of workers and unions to negotiate differentials, that is, separate rates of pay depending on skills. In many areas it took some time to convince the unions that the Liberal reforms really were in their best interests. For the same reason, the labour exchanges, which were introduced by Churchill in 1909, were at first unwelcome to both the unions and the Labour Party.

The policies which Churchill and Lloyd George advocated were a response to the scale of the social problems confronting Edwardian Britain and a positive reaction to Hobson's appeal to the Liberal Party to acknowledge the 'sovereignty of social welfare'. The basic dilemma for the Liberals, however, remained unresolved. In extending the scope of State authority they were challenging the customary Liberal adherence to *laissez-faire* and non-inteference in individual affairs, and at the same time running the risk that their measures would not be acceptable or immediately beneficial to the classes for whom they were intended. The most insistent question raised by contemporaries in regard to welfare reform was where was the money to be found to pay for it. Indeed, it was finance that connected so many of the issues of the time.

Lloyd George always tried to lift the argument above matters of detail by suggesting that the Liberal Government's welfare and financial reforms of the day had all been introduced in pursuit not of petty party interest but of social justice. This approach was an example of his capacity for raising debate to the high moral ground, a skill that he derived from his Nonconformist religious background and one that particularly infuriated those who contrasted his public utterances with the dubious nature of his private life, which had become a matter of widespread rumour and comment around this time.

## A NOTE ON LLOYD GEORGE'S PRIVATE LIFE

In 1912 Lloyd George began his 33 year relationship with Frances Stevenson. As his secretary and lover, Frances Stevenson remained loyal to him for the rest of his life. She became pregnant by him on two occasions, undergoing an abortion in 1915, but giving birth to a daughter, Jennifer, in 1928. During his years as Prime Minister between 1916 and 1922, Frances lived with him at 10 Downing Street and frequently accompanied him on official visits home and abroad. The fact that she was his personal secretary gave a semblance of propriety to their liaison, but it was an open secret that their relationship was more than just professional. His wife Margaret was well aware of the affair, but chose for the sake of the family name to remain discreet. Frances Stevenson and Lloyd George finally married in 1943, two years after Margaret's death. The affair never quite reached the proportions of a public scandal, but in the eyes of critics and opponents it was further evidence of his less than trustworthy character.

A more serious threat to his political career came in 1913 through his implication in the Marconi scandal. It appeared that Lloyd George had used his inside knowledge as Chancellor of the Exchequer to purchase shares in the Marconi Company at the most favourable time, certain that when it was publicly announced that the Company had been awarded a major government contract the shares would leap in value. Although in a subsequent parliamentary enquiry he was officially exonerated from the charge of having acting improperly, the widespread belief remained that he had used his privileged position as a Minister of the Crown to make a killing on the stock market. The whole affair added to his reputation as a public figure who was not entirely honest.

# THE LIBERAL WELFARE REFORMS IN PERSPECTIVE

A question that still arises is whether the policies pursued by the Liberals between 1905 and 1914 constituted an integrated programme or whether they were a series of *ad hoc* responses to particular problems. Lloyd George had made it clear early in the life of the Government that unless the Liberals committed themselves fully to a programme of welfare reform, they might well be superseded by Labour. In 1906 he had declared:

> I have one word for Liberals. I can tell them what will make this ILP [Independent Labour Party] movement a great and sweeping force in this country – a force that will sweep away Liberalism amongst other things. If at the end of an average term of office it were found that a Liberal Parliament had done nothing to cope seriously with the social condition of the people, to remove the national degradation of slums and widespread poverty and destitution in a land glittering with wealth . . . then would a real cry arise in this land for a new party, and many of us here in this room would join in that cry. But if a Liberal Government tackle the landlords, and the brewers, and the peers, as they have faced the parsons, and try to deliver the nation from the pernicious control of this confederacy of monopolists, then the Independent Labour Party will call in vain upon the working men of Britain to desert Liberalism that is so gallantly fighting to rid the land of the wrongs that have oppressed those who labour in it.

Here, it is worth recalling the main elements in the Liberal welfare reforms: old age pensions, labour exchanges and National Insurance. To these should be added the Development Commission set up in 1909 to oversee State investment in welfare. The obvious connection between these innovations does argue that whether or not they were originally intended as such, they did in the event take on the shape of a systematic programme. It may have been rudimentary by later standards, but it did involve a considerable increase in bureaucracy. Rather than creating an overarching welfare state, for which the administrative and financial resources simply did not exist, the Liberals were taking purposeful steps towards what has been termed 'the social service state', a centrally organised attempt to ameliorate the worst of the social and economic deprivation from which large parts of the British population suffered.

Many historians have taken a broader stance. They have argued that it is not possible to view social reform in Britain in isolation. It has to be set against the background of changes in other countries. Modern research supports the idea that social reform was not peculiar to Britain. The commonly-observed phenomenon is that all advanced industrial societies, notwithstanding their varying political structures, have been obliged by the economic consequences of industrialisation to undertake major social and welfare reform. The Liberal initiative in Britain, therefore, was not unique. Historically the question is not why social reform was undertaken but why at that particular time. The answer is that by the early years of the twentieth century, all the political parties were agreed that welfare provision had become a necessity. The obvious case was the Labour Party which had come into being for that very purpose, but even the supposedly reactionary party, the Conservatives, had come to accept the necessity of social reform. In Britain, the history of reform shows that vested interests resist as long as they can, then give way in order to avoid social upheaval. That certainly was why the Conservatives had adopted Joseph Chamberlain's tariff reform programme; it gave them the prospect of acquiring the extra capital to fund welfare without recourse to socially disruptive taxation. What frustrated the Conservatives, therefore, were not the Liberal reforms in themselves but the fact that they were achieved under the free-trade banner.

What we witness before 1914 is a convergence of attitude among the political parties on the question of social reform. They would continue, of course, to engage in the rhetoric of adversarial politics and would indeed differ genuinely in matters of detail, timing and the proper use of resources, but on the necessity of reform itself there was implicit agreement. It is noteworthy that it had been the Conservative Governments of the 1890s which had established the county and county-borough councils, without which the Liberal social legislation of the 1900s could not have been implemented. Social reform required the machinery which had already been set up in the previous decade. The Liberal reforms did not come out of the blue. Significant moves had been made earlier. The scope of local government had been considerably extended; local expenditure on welfare facilities, such as schools and sanitation, had increased by some 300 per cent before 1900. These changes in themselves would not have been enough to deal with social distress, but had they not already been in place the Liberal task would have been that much more difficult.

There was once a commonly held assumption that the Liberal reforms were a response to Labour Party pressure. This view has now been largely discredited. The Labour Party was never strong enough. The Liberals were not dependent on its support before 1910 and, even after the 1910 election when the gap between them and the Unionists had narrowed, it remained inconceivable that the Labour Party would seriously consider voting against the Government since that would have meant its making common cause with the Unionists. It was a fact, acknowledged by the Labour Party itself, that it had made no significant inroad into Liberal Party strength and confidence before 1914.

The idea that Labour represented a socialist alternative to the luke-warm radicalism of the Liberal Government is based on a misunder-standing. The British Labour Party and the trade union movement were not essentially socialist. It is true that some of the more philosophical sections, such as the Fabians, which amalgamated to form the Labour Party, held socialist principles, but the basic objective of the party was not ideological but practical – to improve the working and living conditions of the working classes. This is important to bear in mind for it challenges the notion once popular among earlier historians, who sought to explain the decline of Liberalism by suggesting that it was overtaken in its radicalism by an ideologically-committed Labour Party who were inevitably to seize the Liberal Party's high ground.

The truth is that by 1914 the Liberals, rather than being in irreversible decline, had contained the Unionist challenge, had successfully survived two general elections and had coped with the considerable industrial and social unrest of the pre-1914 period. To speak of the failure of Liberalism by 1914 is to impose on the situation a view which contemporaries would not have recognised. By 1914, the young Labour Party had yet to make any real impression on Liberal strength. It is true that the increased affiliation of the trade unions to the Labour Party gave it an influence outside Parliament, but the trade unions themselves were not yet reckoned as a major political force. The notion that in 1914 the Labour Party was unstoppably and imminently bound to supersede the Liberal

Party would have struck contemporaries as strange. Lloyd George believed that the Labour Party had handicapped itself by attempting to draw its support and strength only from the working class:

[It] is better that you should have a party which combines every section and every shade of opinion, taken from all classes of the community, rather than a party which represents one shade of opinion alone or one class of the community alone . . . Liberals are against anything in the nature of class representation . . . It was a mistake for the Labour Party to go in for anything like independent class representation. They will realize that sooner or later.

| *timeline* | 1906 | Liberals win landslide election victory; Campbell-Bannerman becomes Prime Minister, Lloyd George appointed President of the Board of Trade |
|---|---|---|
| | | Trades Disputes Act passed, reversing Taff Vale decision |
| | | Local authorities empowered to provide school meals |
| | | Merchant Shipping Act, Census of Production Act |
| | | Joseph Chamberlain incapacitated by a stroke |
| | | Lords emasculate the Government's Education Bill |
| | 1907 | Commons accepts Campbell-Bannerman's proposals to limit the Lords' power |
| | | School medical examinations made compulsory and school medical services established |
| | | Rail strike averted by Lloyd George |
| | | Haldane, as War Secretary, begins major reorganisation of British army |
| | 1908 | Asquith becomes Prime Minister, Lloyd George becomes Chancellor of the Exchequer |
| | | Winston Churchill becomes President of the Board of Trade |
| | | Old Age Pensions Act |
| | | Suffragette disturbances |
| | | Lords reject the Government's Licensing Bill |
| | 1909 | Introduction of Navy Bill |
| | | Old Age Pensions Act comes into force |
| | | Under Churchill at Board of Trade, labour exchanges set up; trade boards set up to fix wages in low-paid industries |
| | | Lloyd George introduces his 'People's Budget' |

Lords reject Lloyd George's budget. Lords uphold
Osborne Judgment

1910    General election. Liberals lose seats but continue as a
minority government
Miners strike in Wales
Churchill becomes Home Secretary
Lloyd George Budget passed. Parliament Bill
introduced
Unionists reject Lloyd George's coalition proposal
King promises to create enough peers to pass the
Parliament Bill if the Liberals win the next election
Election
Liberals continue in government

1911    National Insurance Act
Parliament Act finally accepted by the House of
Lords, which loses its power of absolute veto.
Payment of MPs introduced (£400 p.a.)

## Points to consider

1) **In what ways did Lloyd George's work at the Board of Trade and at the Exchequer establish his credentials as an administrator?**

2) **What did Lloyd George mean by describing his 1909 Budget as a 'War Budget'?**

3) **Examine the principles underlying the National Insurance Act of 1911.**

4) **Why was there considerable working-class resistance to the Liberal welfare reforms of this period?**

5) **'Not an integrated programme of social reform, but merely a series of *ad hoc* measures': How accurate is this as a description of the measures introduced by Liberal Governments between 1906 and 1911?**

# 6

# THE LIBERALS AND THE PRE-WAR CRISES, 1911–14

I can imagine no length of resistance to which Ulster will go, which I shall not be ready to support.
*Andrew Bonar Law, the new Conservative leader, addressing his party in 1912*

Vigorous agitation is urged upon lines justified by the position of outlawry to which women are at present condemned.
*The Constitution of the Women's Social and Political Union, 1912*

Let it be understood once and for all that the interests of Capital and Labour are diametrically opposed, and that although it may be necessary for Labour sometimes to acquiesce in 'social peace', such peace is only the lull before the storm.
*The World of Labour, 1913, Socialist writer G.D.H. Cole*

Pre-1914 Britain was a troubled land. The resort to lawlnessness to which these three extracts refer made the period 1911-1914 one of widespread and mounting disturbance. The perceived incapacity of the Liberal Government to withstand the pressures of the times, expressed in the truculence of peers and Ulstermen, suffragettes, and trade unions, is the essence of George Dangerfield's celebrated, if disputed, explanation of the strange death of Liberal England.

## LORDS VERSUS COMMONS

It is difficult to see how a final struggle between Lords and Commons at some point in the early twentieth century could have been avoided. There was a recklessness about the way in which the Lords had rejected or truncated so many of the Liberal measures since 1905, including major licensing and education bills. Even some Unionists were unhappy with the anomaly of an unelected and unrepresentative House being able to destroy legislation that came from the elected assembly. The occasion of the final conflict, when it duly came, was the People's Budget of 1909. Although Lloyd George referred figuratively to his measures as a 'war budget', it is unlikely that he was deliberately spoiling for a fight at that point. He claimed that it was a war to unite not divide the nation.

*The Lords reject the People's Budget, a newspaper headline, 1 December 1909*

However, once the Unionists decided to resist the budget on the grounds that it was an unprecedented attack upon the rights of property, Lloyd George with some relish viewed the whole affair as a chance to turn things to the Liberals' advantage. The Lords and Unionists, by opposing the People's Budget, created a unity among the Liberals. Liberal doubts tended to be overtaken by the basic desire to challenge the forces of reaction. Lloyd George led the Liberal campaign that denounced the peers' unconstitutional attempt to maintain their undemocratic privileges at the expense of the sick and the needy of the nation. He excelled at the art of sarcasm; the House of Lords was not, as the peers claimed, 'the watchdog of the constitution', but 'Mr. Balfour's poodle'. He turned the full force of his invective on those whom he saw as defying the will of the British people.

> Let them [the Lords] realise what they are doing. They are forcing a revolution and they will get it. The Lords may decree revolution, but the people will direct it . . . The question will be asked whether

five hundred men, ordinary men chosen accidentally from among the unemployed, should override the judgement – the deliberate judgement – of millions of people who are engaged in the industry which makes the wealth of the country.

That is one question. Another will be: Who ordained that a few should have the land of Britain as a prerequisite? Who made ten thousand people owners of the soil, and the rest of us trespassers in the land of our birth? Who is it who is responsible for the scheme of things whereby one man is engaged through life in grinding labour to win a bare and precarious subsistence for himself, and when, at the end of his days, he claims at the hands of the community he served a poor pension of eightpence a day, he can only get it through a revolution, and another man who does not toil receives every hour of the day, every hour of the night, whilst he slumbers, more than his poor neighbour receives in a whole year of toil? Where did the table of that law come from? Whose finger inscribed it?

The Lords lost the ensuing battle. In 1910, having eventually and reluctantly allowed Lloyd George's budget through, they were presented with a Parliament Bill, which restricted their delaying power to two years and abolished their absolute veto; it laid down that a Bill sent up by the Commons in three consecutive sessions should become law notwithstanding rejection by the Upper House. For well over a year the Lords resisted fiercely, and succumbed in the end only under the threat of being swamped by 500 specially created Liberal peers. Even then, the majority was a mere 17, achieved by the decision of 37 Conservative peers to vote for the Bill rather than suffer the 'pollution' of their House.

For the sake of historical balance, the argument of the peers who resisted needs to be understood in its contemporary context. The use of the Lords' veto, to block the budget was not simply blind reaction on the part of the Conservatives. They asserted that the only way the free-trade Liberals could pay for their ambitious schemes was by resorting to punitive taxation of the landed class. A government, which in two elections had failed to win an overall majority in the Commons, was attempting to bypass the legitimate constitutional rights of the class under attack by improper use of the budget. What the Liberals had done was tantamount to a declaration of class war. Far from defending privilege, the Lords believed they were speaking for the legal and constitutional freedoms of the nation.

Such an argument may sound unconvincing to the modern ear, but in its time it was sincerely held by its proponents. The 'ditchers' as they were called, those Lords who believed in defending their power of absolute veto to the last ditch, may have been one of history's losing sides, but their argument still commands the historian's attention. Interestingly enough, it was at this juncture that the proposition was first heard that the constitution needed a second chamber with equal power in order to prevent the Commons from becoming an elective tyranny.

**TABLE 7**

| 1910 (Jan/Feb) Election result | Votes | Seats | % vote |
|---|---|---|---|
| Conservatives | 3 127 887 | 273 | 46.9 |
| Liberals | 2 880 581 | 275 | 43.2 |
| Labour | 505 657 | 40 | 7.6 |
| Irish Nationalists | 124 586 | 82 | 1.9 |
| Others | 28 693 | 17 | 0.4 |

Electorate – 7 694 741    Turnout – 86.6%

**TABLE 8**

| 1910 (Dec) Election result | Votes | Seats | % vote |
|---|---|---|---|
| Conservatives | 2 420 566 | 272 | 46.3 |
| Liberals | 2 295 888 | 272 | 43.9 |
| Labour (LRC) | 371 772 | 42 | 7.1 |
| Irish Nationalists | 131 375 | 84 | 2.5 |
| Others | 8 768 | 0 | 0.2 |

Electorate – 7 709 981    Turnout – 81.1%

## THE ULSTER CRISIS

A critical factor in the Peers versus People dispute was the realisation that with the ending of the Lords veto there would be nothing to prevent the Liberals' forcing through Irish Home Rule. Asquith's Government, supported by the Irish Nationalist MPs, could carry the Bill through the Commons, knowing that the Lords could now only delay, not stop, its becoming law. It was the knowledge that they no longer had the constitutional means to block Home Rule that led the Unionists to contemplate illegal action. This heightened the political tension dramatically. It was now not only syndicalist strikers and militant suffragettes who were challenging the rule of law, but Unionists, members of that political and social class who traditionally regarded themselves as the guardians of the law and the upholders of the constitution.

Following Asquith's introduction in 1912 of the third Liberal Home Rule Bill, Ulster prepared for civil war. Asserting that the two elections of 1910 had failed to give the Liberals a mandate to introduce so contentious a measure as Home Rule, the Unionists backed Edward Carson, the leader of the Protestant Covenanters, in a pledge to 'use all means which may be necessary to defeat the setting up of a Home Rule Parliament in Ireland'. By the summer of 1914 two heavily armed forces, Carson's Ulster Volunteers and the nationalist Irish Volunteers, stood ready to confront each other. The difficulty facing Asquith's government was manifest in the so called 'Curragh Mutiny' of March 1914; sympathetic to the Ulster Protestants and influenced by Unionist arguments, a number of British army officers stationed at the Curragh in southern Ireland resigned their commissions to avoid being sent north against the Ulster Volunteers. Asquith persisted in trying to achieve a workable constitutional solution. He proposed an Amending Bill which would suspend the operation of Home Rule in Ulster for six years. This made some headway with the moderate Unionists, but it was the advent of the European war that effected a temporary compromise. In July, with the threat of war against Germany looming ever larger, it was agreed that while the Home Rule Bill would duly become law in September, it would be suspended for the duration of the war. This was by no means a permanent settlement, but it was a respite which allowed the Liberals and Conservatives at Westminster to shelve their differences.

## INDUSTRIAL UNREST

Beyond supporting in Cabinet the right of the Government to send an army into Ulster to keep the peace, Lloyd George was not directly involved in the Irish question at this stage. He was, however, much more concerned with the industrial strife of the time. Although it was exaggerated by those who feared its consequences, there was a syndicalist influence behind some of the strike action of the period. Syndicalism was basically an appeal to the workers to abandon their attempts to improve their conditions by moderate means, and take up all-out disruption, aimed at smashing the industrial-capitalist system. Few workers were interested in the revolutionary philosophy behind syndicalism, but in the charged atmosphere of pre-war Britain the methods it advocated did have an attraction. There were many trade unionists who had been disappointed by the apparent failure of the new Labour Party to redress their grievances. By 1912 the cost of living was 14 per cent higher than in 1906 and unemployment had risen markedly during the same period. Notwithstanding the Liberal welfare measures, the gap between rich and poor was becoming visibly wider. In such circumstances, the call for extra-parliamentary agitation had an appeal for trade unionists, which was reinforced by their belief that legal

## TABLE 9

### Union membership 1900-14

|  | Total No. of Trade Union Members | Total No. of Trade Unions affiliated to TUC | Total No. of members of Trade Unions affiliated to TUC |
|---|---|---|---|
| 1900 | 1 911 000 | 184 | 1 250 000 |
| 1901 | 2 022 000 | 191 | 1 200 000 |
| 1902 | 2 025 000 | 198 | 1 400 000 |
| 1903 | 2 013 000 | 204 | 1 500 000 |
| 1904 | 1 994 000 | 212 | 1 423 000 |
| 1905 | 1 967 000 | 205 | 1 541 000 |
| 1906 | 1 997 000 | 226 | 1 555 000 |
| 1907 | 2 210 000 | 236 | 1 700 000 |
| 1908 | 2 513 000 | 214 | 1 777 000 |
| 1909 | 2 485 000 | 219 | 1 705 000 |
| 1910 | 2 477 000 | 212 | 1 648 000 |
| 1911 | 2 565 000 | – | 2 001 000 |
| 1912 | 3 139 000 | 202 | 1 662 000 |
| 1913 | 3 416 000 | 201 | 2 002 000 |
| 1914 | 4 135 000 | 207 | 2 232 000 |

decisions such as the Osborne Judgement in 1909, which denied the unions the right to use their funds for political purposes, proved that the governing system had an inbuilt hostility to them. The increase in trade union membership around this period may be taken as a measure of the growing frustration of the industrial workers.

Lloyd George believed that his background gave him a natural sympathy for the workers and an understanding of their problems. At the Board of Trade his conciliation had helped to prevent a rail strike in 1907. As a negotiator, he had a gift for appearing to understand all sides of the case; this sometimes led him to promise more than he could deliver, with the result that those parties who felt let down by the final settlement saw him as something of a confidence trickster. This was the risk he took as an arbitrator, but overall his record suggests that his power of personality and his charm (some critics called it his cunning) often broke through stalemate to produce workable settlements. But his skills and energies were greatly taxed in the period 1911-14. He did not accept that the interests of capital and labour were 'diametrically opposed'. Where the strikes of the time were concerned with a demand for higher wages, he was well positioned as Chancellor to mediate between employer and worker. Previously, at the Board of Trade, he had helped in the setting up of conciliation boards and as the strike action that began in 1910 continued to spread he hoped that these might be used as the first step towards bringing the sides together.

The miners, traditionally the most combative of the unions, had already in 1908 won from the Government the legal recognition of a maximum eight-hour day. They now struck for the right to a minimum wage. The strike was particularly serious in South Wales where syndicalist influences were at their strongest. The most disturbing feature for Asquith's Government was the miners' call for sympathetic action throughout the whole industrial workforce. The threat grew larger in the summer of 1912, when three major unions – the dockers, the railwaymen and the seamen – went on strike. Lloyd George managed, however, to persuade the railway workers to end their strike in return for a wage increase and the recognition by the employers of their union rights. To appease the miners, the Government introduced legislation appointing local district wage boards which were responsible for fixing mimimum wages in each region. The strike ended, but the tension remained. By 1914 the miners appeared to be coming together with the dockers and railwaymen, to form a 'triple alliance'. The alliance was unofficial and the three unions did not in fact act in unison. It was this lack of co-ordinated action among the unions rather than government conciliation that prevented the threat of a general strike materialising before 1914. Moreover, as with the Ulster question, the coming of the war in 1914 brought a temporary cessation of strife.

What is particularly notable about the industrial troubles is that the Liberal Government regarded them as so serious as to warrant its involvement in the process of bargaining between bosses and workers. This was another practical example of the Liberals' preparedness to compromise traditional principle. *Laissez-faire* and non-intervention had given way in the face of crisis.

## THE SUFFRAGETTE CRISIS

The question of 'Votes for Women' is now viewed as part of the broader campaign for female emancipation. At the time, whatever their private opinions may have been, politicians approached the matter largely from a party angle. Had they been confident that female suffrage would work to their advantage, they would doubtless have found every reason for supporting it. Their principal concern, however, was the effect that the extension of the franchise would have on their parliamentary strength. This worry applied to them all; none of the parties, Conservative, Liberal or Labour, was completely united on the question. Was the vote to be granted to all women? It was much more likely that it would be given to selected groups only. Labour feared that if this were to happen it would weaken the case for complete male suffrage.

In many ways, the enfranchisement of women might be thought to have been a cause that the new Liberals would eagerly espouse. John Stuart Mill (1806-73), the great Liberal philosopher, had regarded it as a basic requirement in a free society. However, the fine balance between the two main parties (particularly after the elections of 1910) and the incalculable intentions of the potential women voters made a number of the leading Liberals hesitant. Asquith, in particular, strongly resisted the idea. Irritated by the slowness of Parliament to give its attention to the matter, the Women's Social and Political Union (WSPU), founded in 1903 and led by the forceful Emmeline Pankhurst, embarked on a programme of civil disobedience and disruption, a programme that became progressively more violent as the Liberals persisted in their refusal to allocate Government time in Parliament for consideration of the question. Between 1911 and 1914, a series of suffragette outrages that included arson and physical assault, showed the degree of WSPU frustration, but tended to alienate moderate supporters. It also provided an excuse for the Government to introduce penal measures against the suffragettes of a severity that would have been intolerable in less disturbed times. The impasse was no nearer to being resolved when the war intervened in 1914. Mrs. Pankhurst immediately called off the suffragette campaign and committed herself and her followers totally to the war effort.

Lloyd George was, in principle, in favour of votes for women. As an individual MP, he supported the moderate 'suffragist' cause and consistently voted in favour of the private members' bills that were introduced promoting female franchise. But as a minister his reactions were governed by political considerations. His anxiety was that if the extension of the vote was to be made on the principle of some form of property qualification, then only middle class women would be eligible, which electorally would chiefly benefit the Conservatives. For him, it was a question of all or nothing. If women were to gain the vote, it must be all women. As was his way, he negotiated with the various interested groups with a view to reaching a compromise. His motives were not always trusted and he suffered for his pains; in 1912, he was physically assaulted by a group of suffragettes and his house in Surrey was bombed.

'Suffragette Logic', a cartoon of 1911

Lloyd George's major problem as a member of the Cabinet was that although he genuinely tried to find a satisfactory settlement, albeit by means that occasionally appeared devious, his leader, Asquith, refused for too long to give ground to the central principle of female suffrage. The result was that the Liberals did not come out well in the 'Votes for Women' issue. Their apparent reluctance to treat it as a question of principle weakened their moral standing and their failure before 1914 to achieve an acceptable solution proved a political embarrassment.

## CRISIS IN EUROPE

How closely the Liberal Party was attached to the principle of non-intervention in Europe was put to the test in the diplomatic crisis that followed the assassination by Serbian nationalists of Franz Ferdinand, heir to the Austrian throne, in June 1914. A month later a war between Austria and Germany on the one hand and Russia and France on the other seemed imminent. The great question facing Britain was whether she had any legitimate reason or obligation for becoming involved.

A remarkable feature of British foreign policy before 1914 was that it tended to be regarded as the individual concern of the Foreign Secretary. Cabinet scrutiny was unsystematic and, except at times of crisis, seldom demanding. Asquith as Prime Minister was content to leave things to the Foreign Office, with the minimum of interference. Edward Grey had held the position of Foreign Secretary continuously since 1905. By nature a diffident and withdrawn man, he had chosen to act alone and in secret. Reluctant to be drawn into formal commitments, Grey tried to protect British interests by leaving the position deliberately vague. Foreign governments were known to complain that they could never be certain where Britain stood on international questions. The Entente with France, first entered into under Balfour's Government in 1904 and extended into the Triple Entente with the inclusion of Russia in 1907, was specifically not an alliance; at most, it was an understanding rather than a set of agreements. Since, therefore, Britain in 1914 was not formally committed to any of the European states involved in the crisis, no one could be sure, not even the Cabinet, what her obligations actually were.

Given the secrecy of Grey's diplomacy since 1905 and the consequent uncertainty of Britain's diplomatic position, it is little wonder that there were considerable divisions within the Cabinet over the question of entering the war. The Liberal Party, with its strong non-interventionist traditions in foreign policy, did not immediately incline to war. Since Britain lacked formal commitment to either France or Russia, it would require a specific issue to tilt the balance in favour of war. That issue, Grey believed, came in the form of Belgian neutrality. It was Germany's violation of that neutrality by sending her armies through Belgium in order to attack France that united the Cabinet and the nation after their initial wavering. Writing in retrospect in the 1920s Grey argued:

> The real reason for going into the war was that, if we did not stand by France and stand up for Belgium against this aggression, we should be isolated, discredited, and hated; and there would be before us nothing but a miserable and ignoble future.

Grey wrote his postwar analysis in order to establish that it had been with the highest of motives that the Liberal Government had taken Britain into what was to prove a struggle of unimagined suffering and destruction. He presented the defence of Belgium as having been the great moral purpose which animated the nation in 1914, and it is certainly true that it was the announcement of Germany's formal rejection of Britain's demand that Belgian independence be honoured that rallied the Commons in favour of Britain's declaration of war. This argument, however, becomes somewhat compromised when set against other admissions by Grey.

> We felt that to stand aside would mean the domination of Germany; the subordination of France and Russia; the isolation of Britain . . . and ultimately that Germany would wield the whole power of the Continent.

This definition of what Grey called 'the true issue' is instructive. Britain, he said, could not stand aside and permit the German domination of Europe. This, it should be noted, was a consideration that applied prior to and regardless of the German occupation of Belgium. Effective though the image of an idealistic Britain crusading to defend gallant little Belgium was in convincing waverers that this was the reason for Britain's going to war, the true motivation was altogether more self-interested. In keeping with tradition and, indeed, with Grey's own aims since 1905, Britain was not prepared to tolerate one nation upsetting the balance of power in Europe, thereby endangering her own security. It is difficult to see the issue of Belgian neutrality as anything other than a pretext for war. All the probabilities were that Britain would have gone to war with France against Germany in 1914 irrespective of the Belgian issue. The interventionist argument had prevailed.

Prior to 1914, Lloyd George's attention to foreign affairs tended to be spasmodic. This is understandable in view of his preoccupation with domestic matters. As Chancellor, his interest in overseas matters was largely dictated by financial considerations. If a particular policy entailed increased expenditure, he was naturally involved. He was faced with the difficulty that has confronted all twentieth-century chancellors but weighs more heavily on those with a Liberal conscience – how to balance the rival claims of welfare and defence expenditure. The armed-service chiefs continually pressed for increased resources; the Admiralty was particularly insistent in its demand for the building of more Dreadnoughts, the great battleships, that represented Britain's naval strength. The Admiralty's argument was that Germany's growing warship programme was a direct threat to British security and had to be countered by an equivalent expansion of the Royal Navy's strength. Lloyd George fought a running battle with Reginald McKenna, the First Lord of the Admiralty, and John Fisher, the fanatically committed First Sea Lord, to reduce the naval estimates.

He had a similar struggle with Richard Haldane, the War Secretary, whose reforms of the army required increased expenditure. What is significant is that in the end Lloyd George invariably managed to find the money for the proposed military projects. This does suggest that, along with most of Asquith's Cabinet, he took the German threat seriously. As was noted when analysing his attitude to the Anglo-Boer War, Lloyd George was certainly not a pacifist. He had opposed that war because he considered it unnecessary, but he was not one of those Liberals who held to non-intervention on principle. If Britain's legitimate interests were genuinely involved, he was prepared to accept the case for war.

He had given clear signals of his attitude towards Germany in 1911. In a widely reported speech delivered at the Mansion House in London, he warned the German government against taking an aggressive stance in foreign affairs and stated the case for possible British intervention:

> I believe it is essential in the highest interests, not merely of this
> country, but of the world, that Britain should at all hazards
> maintain her place and prestige amongst the Great Powers . . . if a
> situation were to be forced on us, in which peace could only be
> preserved by . . . allowing Britain to be treated . . . as if she were of
> no account in the Cabinet of nations, then I say emphatically that
> peace at that price would be a humiliation intolerable for a great
> country like ours to endure.

The difficulty for Lloyd George, and one that further illustrated the
divisions within Liberalism, was that his acceptance of Britain's right to
intervene put him at variance with those Liberals who hitherto had been
his staunchest supporters, those of the radical, Nonconformist tradition,
who regarded war as an unacceptable option in British foreign policy.

Lloyd George's precise attitude at the time of the Government's
decision to declare war is not entirely clear. Official records of the
Cabinet's discussions were not kept; we have to rely on the subsequent
comments of those involved. At one point he appears to have been
willing to resign from the Cabinet and oppose the war, should Germany
draw back from violating Belgium. But there is reason to doubt his
sincerity. His closest confidante at the time, Frances Stevenson, wrote in
her diary account that Lloyd George's mind was already made up in
favour of war and that the invasion of Belgium simply provided a
'heaven-sent excuse for supporting a declaration of war'. He himself
later said that what helped persuade him to support the declaration of
war was the urgent clamour for war that he witnessed among the
ordinary people as he drove through the crowded streets of London.

## THE CRISES IN PERSPECTIVE

Considerable attention has been paid to the crises and tensions that
occurred in Britain between 1910 and 1914. It is tempting with hindsight
to look back upon the period between 1910 as a sunset or golden age,
before Britain was overwhelmed by a series of domestic and foreign
crises that culminated in the outbreak of a ruinous war that was to

destroy what remained of the old world. There is also a theory, once quite fashionable, that what happened in Britain in the years immediately before 1914 was part of a general world crisis that saw political and social upheaval in all the continents. The theory was largely a product of the Marxist hypothesis that the collapse of capitalism would be accompanied by a series of desperate struggles as the ruling classes worldwide tried unavailingly to cling on to power. Interesting though the notion remains, the evidence is too diffuse to substantiate it as a working theory. That similar events occur simultaneously does not prove a connection between them. The variation in local circumstances is too wide for a common cause to apply to them all.

The seriousness of the disputes over the House of Lords and over Home Rule give the impression that the period was one of major conflict between the parties. In one sense this was obviously true, yet one of the most significant features of the time was Lloyd George's belief in the possibility of achieving compromise or consensus between Liberals and Unionists. He had realistic grounds for this. In 1910, after the first general election resulted in a hung parliament, some among the more progressive Conservatives, such as Leo Amery and J. L. Garvin, judged that Lloyd George's commitment to the Liberals was less than absolute and that he might therefore be willing to join a two-party coalition on an agreed programme of social reform and Home Rule. Lloyd George was attracted by the idea and made a number of attempts to carry it further. Although the notion proved premature, since the Conservative leader Balfour rejected it, what it had shown was both Lloyd George's accommodating turn of mind and the degree of concurrence between the parties on certain central issues.

Of late, historians have seen more significance in the episode than was allowed by earlier writers. Now that the period is no longer exclusively interpreted as a struggle between capital and labour, it is possible to give greater weight to the idea of the parties' having had more in common than divided them. Tactical flexibility is a more evident characteristic of British political parties than ideological consistency. Lloyd George suggested that membership of one of the parties was not a final definition of an individual's politics. Angered by the sniping at him by the less progressive elements within his party, he observed to a colleague in 1911:

I don't know exactly what I am, but I'm sure I'm not a Liberal. They have no sympathy with the people ... All down History, nine-tenths of mankind have been grinding the corn for the remaining one-tenth, and been paid with the husks – and bidden to thank God they had the husks ... As long as I was settling disputes with their workmen, which they had not got enough sense to settle themselves, these great Business Men said I was the greatest Board of Trade President of modern times. When I tried to do something for the social welfare of their workmen, they denounced me as a Welsh thief.

| timeline | | |
|---|---|---|
| | 1911 | Strikes by dockers, seamen and railway workers |
| | Oct | Churchill becomes First Lord of the Admiralty |
| | Nov | Andrew Bonar Law replaces Balfour as leader of the Unionist Party |
| | | Serious suffragette disturbances in London |
| | 1912 Feb | Miners strike for a minimum wage |
| | Mar | A Bill introduced to establish minimum wages for miners |
| | Apr | End of miners' strike; introduction of third Irish Home Rule Bill |
| | May | London dock strike |
| | Aug | End of dock strike |
| | Sept | 'Solemn Covenant' opposing Home Rule signed by 200,000 Ulstermen |
| | | Anglo-French naval convention |
| | 1913 Jan | Home Rule Bill rejected by House of Lords |
| | July | Home Rule Bill again rejected by Lords |
| | Oct | Lloyd George begins his 'Land Campaign' for reform of social conditions in the countryside |
| | | Trade Union Act reverses the Osborne Judgement |
| | 1914 | 'Triple Alliance' of miners, railwaymen and dockers unions |
| | Mar | Suffragette riots in London |
| | | Curragh 'Mutiny' in Ireland, when officers in British army resign their commission rather than fight against Ulstermen |
| | May | Third readings of Home Rule Bill and Welsh Church Disestablishment Bill |
| | June | Assassination of Franz Ferdinand in Sarajevo |

| July | Failure of Buckingham Palace Conference to reach compromise over Ulster question |
| Aug | Britain declares war on Germany |

## *Points to consider*

1) **Why did the House of Lords eventually vote for the restriction of its own constitutional powers?**
2) **Did the Liberals have a mandate to introduce the Home Rule Bill in 1912?**
3) **How far was Lloyd George's response to the pre-war industrial unrest in keeping with Liberal principles?**
4) **Why was Asquith's Government reluctant to accept the principle of 'Votes for Women'?**
5) **How crucial was the Belgian issue in the Liberal Government's decision to declare war on Germany in 1914?**
6) **Was the Liberal Party stronger or weaker as a result of the crises of 1911-14?**

# 7

# THE LIBERALS AND THE WAR, 1914–16

## THE LIBERAL RESPONSE TO WAR

The 1914-18 war had profound effects on British politics in general and the Liberal Party in particular. The struggle against Germany became a total war. It involved an unprecedented extension of State authority that completely overrode the free-trade, non-interventionist theories of old-style liberalism. Notions of individual freedom and limited State authority meant little in the face of the State's claim to direct the lives of its people.

War was a great challenge to Liberal values. Once Liberals had in practice accepted the necessity and, therefore, the validity of the declaration of war on Germany, they had somehow to transmute their old values. The powerful anti-war feelings expressed at the time of the Boer War now had to be modified to accommodate the spirit of patriotism necessary to sustain the war effort. Rationing, conscription and the extension of State authority in many areas of the economy were responses to the needs of waging total war. The old Liberal virtues of personal freedom, peace and retrenchment were impossible to preserve uncompromised in war time. The simple truth was that the pressure of war rendered such values philosophical luxuries that the nation could not afford. Survival was the prime objective.

The Liberal dilemma was expressed in the very first measure necessitated by the war. In August 1914, Parliament rushed through the Defence of the Realm Act (DORA), which granted the State and its agencies extensive powers over the lives of ordinary citizens. This measure was re-enacted a number of times during the course of the war, on each occasion greatly extending the authority of the State. A whole range of restrictions followed, including press censorship, limitations on the flow of information, checks on the freedom to travel, and regulations that denied workers the right to change jobs and dictated to employers in their choice of workers.

## LLOYD GEORGE AS WARTIME CHANCELLOR

The pacifist element among the Liberals hoped that Lloyd George might lead an anti-war faction in the party or even in the government. He soon disappointed them. Whatever may have been his uncertainties about entering the war, once Britain was engaged his commitment to it was total. One remarkable feature was that the political truce, which the parties agreed to for the duration of the war, allowed Lloyd George to develop his ideas of consensus politics. He was an advocate of inter-party discussion and from the beginning of the war strongly urged Asquith to consider broadening the basis of his Government.

The outbreak of hostilities brought no immediate change in the structure of the Government, but as it became increasingly clear that the war was going to be a much more protracted affair than originally anticipated the pressure for change mounted. Asquith was as patriotic as the next man, but his calm demeanour and refusal to be panicked into rash action, attributes which had proved highly effective during the pre-1914 domestic crises, now appeared to suggest a lack of dynamism, if not of commitment.

In contrast, Lloyd George's bustling energy seemed ideally suited to wartime needs. His two wartime budgets in 1914 and 1915 doubled income tax and greatly increased Government expenditure. Gone was the restraint he had shown when trying to hold in check the pre-1914 defence estimates. His skills as a negotiator produced one of the most important social contracts of the war, the Treasury Agreement of 1915. This was a settlement that enlisted the trade unions as an essential component in the war effort. In return for accepting non-strike agreements and 'dilution', the employment of unskilled men and women in jobs previously restricted to skilled workers, the unions were guaranteed improved wages and conditions. The real significance of the Treasury Agreement lay not in its details but in its recognition of the trade unions as essential partners in the war effort. They were now participants in the functioning of the State; they could no longer be regarded as outsiders. Lloyd George called the Treasury Agreement 'the great charter for labour'.

## THE ASQUITH COALITION, 1915-16

The implicit understanding that underlay the political truce agreed to by the political parties in 1914 was that Asquith's Government would conduct the war in a way that was acceptable to them all. By May 1915, however, serious criticism had begun to be made of Asquith's performance as war leader. As might be expected, the strongest objections came from the Conservatives who, unlike the Labour and Irish parties, had never had any doubts about the necessity of Britain's going to war. The critical shell shortage and the failure of the Gallipoli campaign (see page 77) were the main pretexts for the Conservative demand for a government shake-up. Asquith gave way before the pressure and accepted that the seriousness of the war situation necessitated the formation of a coalition government. Bonar Law, Curzon, Balfour and Carson were among the leading Conservatives who received government posts.

From Lloyd George's point of view, the formation of the coalition was welcome in that it provided the opportunity to advance the principle of centre politics. From 1914 he had encouraged Asquith to use the truce agreed between the parties as a means of widening the political base of the Government. Lloyd George acted as something of a political broker after 1914. It was to him rather than Asquith to whom Bonar Law turned in 1915 when considering the prospect of coalition between the parties. Lloyd George's pre-1914 record helped in this respect; his approaches to the Conservatives concerning a possible coalition at the time of the impasse over the Lords had suggested that consensus politics figured genuinely in his scheme of things.

The prospect of a coalition was especially appealing to Bonar Law. It offered his party a return to government office after ten frustratingly powerless years, this without the necessity of a general election which should have occured in 1915, an election which the Conservatives judged they had little hope of winning. In marked contrast to Conservative elation was the depression that the Coalition created in many Liberals. They felt the party had compromised its principles by allowing the Conservatives back into office, albeit at first only in minor positions. Moreover, the Coalition, as they saw it, was really a face-saving exercise for Asquith, a way of hiding how badly the war effort was going under his less than inspiring direction.

In the Cabinet reshuffle that accompanied the formation of the Coalition, Lloyd George moved from the Exchequer to head the newly created Ministry of Munitions. There were contemporaries who initially viewed this appointment as a demotion. He soon proved them wrong. His move to Munitions gave him the freedom to develop a new department untrammelled by restrictive civil service traditions. He was able to make the Ministry a model of what could be achieved when a government department devoted itself solely to the task in hand, free from the usual political restraints. His essential aim was to produce more shells, the lack of which had become the chief complaint in the mounting criticism of Asquith's handling of the war. Ably served by loyal departmental officials and advised by a series of experts drawn from outside politics, Lloyd George had outstanding success in increasing the production of armaments. One particular statistic illustrates this; when the war began the army possessed 1,330 machine guns, by the time it ended it had a quarter of a million. Moreover, by 1918, the supply of shells had begun to exceed demand. Lloyd George ascribed this success

---

# LLOYD GEORGE SHELLS

An officer of the Durhams, who took part in the battle of Hooge, has written to a friend at Hitchen, describing the final charge, and adds:-

"It was the new Lloyd George shells which gave us the heart to make the charge, after being so heavily hit. These new shells are magnificent and after our fellows got into the captured trenches they gave three cheers for Lloyd George."

*From the Caernarvon and Denbigh Herald, 27 August 1915*

---

to the fact that the Ministry was 'from first to last a business-man organisation'. His use of experts from the areas of industrial production and supply was a step towards his concept of a government of national efficiency, drawing from a pool of the best talents and subordinating party politics to the needs of the nation.

As 1915 wore on and the war threatened increasingly to be a protracted one, requiring enormous resources in manpower, it became clear that the existing system of voluntary enlistment would not be sufficient to keep the army up to strength. Something approaching a national campaign, led principally by the Conservatives, had developed by the autumn; it demanded that in the hour of the nation's need able-bodied men should be compulsorily called up for military service. After trying to evade the issue by suggesting various alternatives short of conscription, Asquith eventually bowed to pressure and supported the Military Service Act, introduced in January 1916, which provided for the compulsory enlistment of males between the ages of 18 and 41. A group of 50 Liberals voted against the bill on the grounds that it was an unprecedented invasion of the liberty of the citizen to oblige him to engage in warfare. The majority of Liberals sympathised with this view but, nonetheless, voted for the Bill, believing that circumstances made it necessary. It was this acceptance of the argument from necessity that fatally compromised liberalism as a political philosophy.

Conscription caused dissension in the Cabinet. Grey and McKenna were among those who were strongly against it. Lloyd George, however, true to his conviction that the war justified extraordinary measures in mobilising the nation, threatened to resign if it were not introduced. He also objected to the concession written into the Act that allowed exemption from war service for conscientious objectors. How far his authoritarianism stretched was later shown in 1918 when, against Bonar Law's plea that the Conscription Act should never be used 'as an agent in an industrial dispute', Lloyd George helped Churchill break a strike among munitions workers in Leeds by threatening to send the strikers straight to the war front.

What added to the significance of the affair was that the strike had begun as a protest by the workers at their being transferred against their wishes from one factory to another. Little of the radicalism of Lloyd George's pro-Boer years seemed to have survived. Notwithstanding the gains undoubtedly made by the unions during the war in regard to status and the negotiating of better wage deals, there was a strong and often-voiced feeling among the workers that on both the home and war fronts the burden of winning the war was falling disproportionately on them. They were the class that was having to make the greatest sacrifice, and they doubted that Lloyd George, despite the many tributes he paid them in his public speeches, was as understanding of this as he should have been.

## LLOYD GEORGE AS WAR MINISTER, 1916

Despite his own success as Minister of Munitions, Lloyd George became increasingly depressed during 1916 by the military ineffectiveness of the Allied war effort. Lloyd George was an 'Easterner', the term applied to those who believed that the stalemate on the Western front could be broken by mounting major diversionary campaigns on other fronts, which would force the Central Powers (Germany, Austria-Hungary, and their allies) to stretch their resources to breaking point. The Gallipoli campaign in 1915, championed by Winston Churchill, involving an attack upon Germany's south-eastern ally, Turkey, was the outstanding example of this form of strategy. Tragically, Gallipoli proved a disastrous failure. Even though it could be argued that it was the tactics of that particular campaign that were to blame rather than the strategic concept behind it, the whole Easterner case was undermined for the rest of the war. This gave weight to Chief-of-Staff Haig and the other generals who asserted that the only way to defeat Germany was by the deployment of massive force on the Western Front; hence their demand for ever more manpower and resources to continue their war of attritition in Europe.

This put Lloyd George in a difficult position and he began seriously to consider resigning from the Government. What prevented him from doing so was one of those quirks of fate that dramatically altered his own position and had a profound effect on the eventual outcome of the war. On 5 June 1916, Lord Kitchener, the War Secretary, was drowned at sea after the ship on which he was travelling to Russia struck a mine off Scapa Flow. It had originally been planned that Lloyd George would accompany Kitchener on what was intended as a visit to raise Russian morale, but he had had to withdraw because of his close involvement in the crisis discussions that followed the Easter Rising (see page 98). This change of plan both saved Lloyd George's life and led to his taking the post that Kitchener had held.

He became War Minister five days after the launching of the British offensive on the Somme, the most costly single campaign ever fought by a British army in any war. On the first day of battle, 1 June 1916, Britain suffered 57,000 casualties; by the time the offensive had petered out four months later that figure had risen to 420,000. At first Lloyd George, believing the estimates that the generals gave him, supported the offensive, but when it became evident that the Somme was a deadly strategic miscalculation, he turned bitterly against General Haig, the Commander-in-Chief of the British armies in France, and Sir William Robertson, Chief of the Imperial General Staff. From the autumn of 1916 he was at loggerheads with the military.

Lloyd George brought to the War Ministry the same energy and dynamism that had characterised his work at Munitions. His achievement as an organiser increased rather than lessened the tensions between him and the generals. He came to believe that it was their incompetence that was limiting Britain's success in the war. He could not accept that they were planning adequately or using their resources effectively. His initial idea was that the removal of the more inept commanders, Robertson being a particular target since technically he was Lloyd George's superior at the War Ministry, would be the means of improving the war effort.

## THE CHALLENGE TO ASQUITH, 1916

Lloyd George's exasperation with the military soon expanded into the belief that what was needed was a much more committed political leadership. He proposed, therefore, the setting up of a three-man war council with himself as its chairman. This was not simple arrogance. He considered that his experience and achievements at Munitions and as War Minister indicated that he, more than any other civilian politician, both understood and represented the expectations of the nation. He claimed that he knew the people and the people knew him. He seems also to have genuinely believed that Asquith's duties as Prime Minister were so heavy that it was unreasonable to expect him to be able to dedictate himself solely to the task of prosecuting the war.

The Conservatives proved eager to support Lloyd George's initiative. They had never been fully content with Asquith as war leader, even after the formation of the Coalition in May 1915. Bonar Law and Edward Carson let Lloyd George know that they were prepared to back him against Asquith. A series of complicated manoeuvres followed in the autumn of 1916. The key question was whether Asquith would be willing to allow the proposed war council to function without him. In the end, judging that this would be too great an infringement of his authority as Prime Minister, he insisted that he must be the head of the council. Lloyd George offered his resignation, whereupon the Conservatives informed Asquith that they were not willing to serve in a Coalition government if Lloyd George was not a member. What helped tip the balance was that Lloyd George could count on his side all the major national newspapers. He numbered among his friends at least five of the leading editors or proprietors. This proved of obvious political value to him. (It is noteworthy that when he lost their support, as he largely did after 1918, he was deprived of a major source of political influence). In 1916 only the *Daily News* unequivocally supported Asquith. It was an article in the *Times*, asserting that the Prime Minister was 'unfit to be fully charged with the supreme direction of the war' that appears to have finally broken Asquith's resistance.

The leadership crisis in December 1916 revealed that Asquith had no natural allies. The willingness of the Labour Party to support him earlier had reflected a commitment to the war effort generally rather than to Asquith personally, while the Irish MPs had largely lost interest in English domestic politics following the Easter Rising. More significantly for the future of the Liberal Party, some 130 Liberal MPs declared their readiness to follow Lloyd George. It is possible to view this as marking the final great divide between old and new style Liberalism. Indeed, some historians have interpreted it as part of the class politics of the time, a revolt of the former outsiders in British politics against the existing political establishment. For example, A.J.P. Taylor writes:

> The Liberal leaders associated with Asquith, were men of excessive refinement . . . Lloyd George's supporters were rougher in origin and in temperament: mostly Radical nonconformists and self-made men . . . None was a banker, merchant, or financial magnate; none a Londoner. Theirs was a long-delayed revolt of the

provinces against London's political and cultural dominance: a revolt on behalf of the factories and workshops where the war was being won.

Opponents believed that it was Lloyd George's desire for personal power that led him to bring Asquith down. Modern scholarship, however, tends strongly to view this as a myth. The truth is Lloyd George was never in a strong enough position to plot Asquith's downfall. It was the refusal of the Conservatives to remain loyal to Asquith that made all the difference. By 1916, Lloyd George may well have been less than satisfied with Asquith's leadership, but he could not have removed Asquith simply by his own efforts; it was the Conservatives who were responsible for making it impossible for Asquith to continue. It is also the case that Asquith must share some of the blame for his own downfall. Throughout the political crisis, he was blind to the larger issues involved. He seems never to have understood the sincerity of those who opposed him, regarding their behaviour as a betrayal of him personally rather than a genuine attempt to halt Britain's declining war fortunes.

| *timeline* | 1914 Aug | Outbreak of war. |
|---|---|---|
| | | Defence of the Realm Act |
| | | Lloyd George introduces first war budget |
| | 1915 March | Treasury Agreement with the unions |
| | April | Beginning of Gallipoli campaign |
| | May | Formation of Coalition Government under Asquith – Lloyd George appointed Munitions Minister, Bonar Law becomes Colonial Secretary, Balfour replaces Churchill at the Admiralty, Curzon becomes Lord Privy Seal |
| | Dec | Robertson appointed Commander of Imperial General Staff. Haig becomes British Commander-in-Chief on the Western Front |
| | 1916 Jan | Allies evacuate Gallipoli peninsula. Introduction of conscription. |
| | April | Easter Rising in Dublin suppressed. |
| | May | Lloyd George negotiates with Carson and Redmond over Ireland |
| | June | Naval battle at Jutland establishes British naval superiority. |

| | |
|---|---|
| July–Nov | Battle of the Somme |
| July | Lloyd George made Secretary for War. |
| Dec | Conservatives withdraw support from Asquith, who resigns; Lloyd George becomes Prime Minister and forms new Coalition Government. |

## Points to consider

1) **What particular political problems did the onset of war in 1914 create for the Liberal Party?**
2) **Examine the view that the 1915-16 Coalition advantaged the Conservatives but compromised the Liberals.**
3) **In what sense was Lloyd George an 'Easterner'?**
4) **How far was Asquith the author of his own misfortunes in December 1916?**

# 8

# LORD GEORGE AS WARTIME PRIME MINISTER, 1916–18

After 1918, Lloyd George was frequently referred to as 'the man who won the war'. No one person, of course, can win a modern war, but as a reference to the inspiration he brought to bear as Prime Minister it is a fitting tribute to the scale of his contribution. At the time he took over as Premier late in 1916 British morale was entering its lowest trough of the war. The intensifying of the German U-Boat (submarine) campaign early in 1917, sinking ships and interrupting supplies of food and raw materials, put a barely tolerable strain on Britain's resources. There was talk of a compromise peace and defeatism was in the air. Lloyd George's refusal even at this darkest hour to contemplate other than total victory inspired his colleagues, reassured the waverers, and put heart into the nation. It was characteristic of him that, having argued previously that the duties of the premiership were too burdensome to allow the Prime Minister to run the war effort, Lloyd George proceeded to combine those two functions when he became Prime Minister himself.

## LLOYD GEORGE AND THE MILITARY

It was to be expected that his dynamism would intensify his conflict with the military. They objected to what they regarded as a civilian politician attempting to decide questions of strategy. For his part, Lloyd George rejected as wholly unreasonable the idea that the generals should make their demands for huge numbers of men and vast amounts of material without being directly answerable to the Government for the use they made of them. It was a question of who was ultimately responsible for running the war. This dispute has sometimes been portrayed as a struggle to decide whether Britain in wartime was to be governed by politicians or generals. There are writers who see Lloyd George as having saved Britain from becoming a military dictatorship, but only at the price of its becoming a political one.

Lloyd George never wavered in his resolution to carry on the war to complete victory no matter how long it took. At the same time, he was appalled by the scale of the slaughter and believed that there had to be alternatives to the mass offensives which seemed the only strategy the generals were willing to consider. He spent a great deal of his time as Prime Minister trying to outwit the generals without at the same time weakening the war effort overall. Part of his technique was deliberately to keep the army under-resourced while maintaining that his Government was making every effort to meet the demands of the service chiefs. His hope was that this would force the generals to reconsider their unimaginative strategy of mass attack. His success in persuading the Admiralty in 1917 to adopt the convoy system as the main defence against the depradations wreaked on merchant shipping by the German U-boats showed what could be achieved militarily when imagination and new thinking were given a chance. Lloyd George also outflanked Haig by a series of manoeuvres in 1917 that resulted in Marshal Foch, the French Commander-in-Chief, taking supreme command of the joint allied forces in western Europe.

## LLOYD GEORGE'S METHODS AS PRIME MINISTER

Under Lloyd George's leadership after 1916, the centralising tendencies that had come with the war became more pronounced. To retain central direction and control of the new state agencies, a special Cabinet Secretariat was set up under the leadership of Maurice Hankey. Still more significant was the adoption by Lloyd George as Prime Minister of his own private secretariat, directly responsible to him as head of the War Cabinet. Known as 'the Garden Suburb', because it was housed in a makeshift building in the gardens of 10 Downing Street, this secretariat was made up of a group of advisers and experts in constant touch with the Prime Minister. Lloyd George justified its existence by his need to be in immediate day-to-day contact with the constantly changing war situation; it made possible the instant decision making demanded by the war.

## THE NEW CONDUCTOR.

OPENING OF THE 1917 OVERTURE.

Others were more dubious about its purpose and effects. The workings of the secretariat appeared to them to detach government even further from ministerial involvement and parliamentary scrutiny. Lloyd George seldom attended Parliament between 1916 and 1918. By relying increasingly on outside experts rather than elected politicians, he appeared to some observers to be abandoning the traditional methods of parliamentary government. Critics suggested that Lloyd George was turning the British premiership into an American-style presidency; some even went so far as to accuse him of adopting the methods of a dictator. The Liberal journalist, H. W. Massingham, described the purpose of the secretariat as being:

> to protect a powerful Chief from the interference of ordinary politicians, including Ministers and the heads of public depart-ments. The Chief was thus saved from frivolous interruptions in his pursuit of far-reaching designs and gained in power ... by a mysterious aloofness, like a juggernaut hidden in a secret shrine into which no alien may gaze.

By the end of the war an increase in state power had occurred that would have been unimaginable, let alone acceptable, in peacetime. Large areas of British industry were under central control, as was all public transport. Military conscription, food rationing and controls on profits and wages and on working hours were among the outstanding examples of the powers that the Asquith and Lloyd George Govern-ments had taken unto themselves. Lloyd George's revolutionary People's Budget of 1909 seemed oddly restrained in retrospect, when compared with the wartime budgets that raised income tax from 6d (2½p) to 6s (30p) in the pound and introduced super-tax on annual incomes over £2,500. Wine, spirits, and tobacco were taxed and Lloyd George aroused widespread unpopularity by his introduction of licensing laws which severely restricted the opening hours of public houses. He sincerely believed that the excessive drinking habits of the British workers lowered production and weakened the war effort. In a characteristic statement, which recalled the Welsh temperance background of his youth, he declared: 'This country is facing three enemies – Germany, Austria and drink – and the deadliest of these is drink!'.

In 1917 alone, the worst year of the war for Britain, six new ministries came into being: Blockade, Food, Labour, National Service, Pensions and Shipping. 1918 saw the establishment of the Air Ministry and the Ministry of Reconstruction. This growth in government power necessitated a huge extension of State bureaucracy. The civil service, in terms of personnel and premises, underwent a rapid expansion. In the face of these developments, the traditional Liberal suspicion of bureaucracy was swept aside in the rush to adapt Britain's institutions to the needs of war.

These measures were justified by reference to the requirements of national survival, but they constituted a significant challenge to the concept of individual liberty. There were Liberals who protested. They were usually the same people who had opposed the declaration of war; their voice, however, sounded faintly against the general clamour for war and for the reorganisation of society that the war effort demanded. Lloyd George declared:

> a perfectly democratic State has the right to commandeer every resource, every power, life, limb, wealth, and everything else for the interest of the state.

It was such developments that the anti-war group of Liberals had feared in 1914; they had joined members of the Labour Party in forming the Union of Democratic Control, a pressure group that protested against the war and urged a negotiated peace. Even those Liberals who had supported the war from the first realised the difficulty of preserving their original ideals in the face of the fundamental changes that were being brought about by the war. Of necessity, British government during the war became essentially illiberal. DORA, restrictions on free trade and the introduction of conscription were outstanding examples of a whole series of measures and regulations which Asquith's and Lloyd George's Governments felt obliged to introduce. The Liberal State at war was very different from the Liberal State at peace.

## THE COUPON ELECTION

In a reversal of what had happened to him two years earlier, Asquith in the summer of 1918 led an attack on Lloyd George's handling of the war. The point at issue was a product of the Prime Minister's long-running conflict with the military. In May 1918, General Maurice, the former Director of Military Operations, publicly accused Lloyd George of deliberately distorting the figures of troop strength in order to suggest that the British army in France was stronger than it actually was. Maurice's aim was to prove that it was not the army leaders, but the Government, who were responsible for Britain's failure to win a decisive breakthrough on the Western Front. Asquith, taking the side of the generals, used his accusation as the basis for proposing a parliamentary vote of no confidence in the Coalition Government. Lloyd George responded effectively, albeit not altogether honestly, by claiming that the figures he had originally quoted had been provided by Maurice himself. Asquith did not acquit himself very ably in the Commons' debate that followed. He lost the initiative and the House divided 293:106 in favour of Lloyd George. The result left Asquith and his supporters looking like a group of malcontents who had irresponsibly sought to embarrass the Government at a time of great national danger.

Politically, the importance of the Maurice debate was that it destroyed the chance of Liberal reunification. Asquith's attack on the Government's policy may not have been personally motivated but it showed how wide the gap had grown between himself and Lloyd George. It deepened the divide between the two factions in the Liberal Party and gave shape to politics for the next four years. Those who opposed Lloyd George in the debate were those who would stand as official Liberal Party candidates against him in the 1918 general election. Bonar Law and Lloyd George agreed to continue their coalition into peacetime. A joint letter carrying both their signatures was sent to all those candidates who were willing to declare themselves supporters of the Coalition. This written endorsement became known as 'the coupon', a wry reference to the ration coupons introduced during the war, and led to the election being referred to as 'the Coupon Election'.

Judged purely as the achievement of a short-term political aim, the election was a remarkable success for Lloyd George and the Coalitionists (see Table 10 page 88).

However, in the light of later developments which saw the Liberal Party decline into impotence, it can be argued that Lloyd George's decision to perpetuate the Liberal split by carrying the Coalition into peacetime, permanently destroyed any chance the Liberal Party had of ever genuinely reuniting and recovering. Kenneth Morgan describes the

**TABLE 10**

| 1918 Election Result | Votes | Seats | % vote |
|---|---|---|---|
| Coalition Unionist | 3 504 198 | 335 | 32.6 |
| Coalition Liberal | 1 455 640 | 133 | 13.5 |
| Coalition Labour | 161 521 | 10 | 1.5 |
| (Coalition totals) | (5 121 259) | (478) | (47.6) |
| Conservatives | 370 375 | 23 | 3.4 |
| Liberals | 1 298 808 | 28 | 12.1 |
| Labour | 2 385 472 | 63 | 22.2 |
| Irish Nationalists | 238 477 | 7 | 2.2 |
| Others | 572 503 | 10 | 5.3 |

Electorate – 21 392 322      Turnout – 58.9%

coupon election as 'the greatest of disasters for the Liberal Party and the greatest of tragedies for Lloyd George'. This modern estimation reinforces the view expressed nearer the time by Herbert Gladstone, the former Liberal Chief Whip:

> The result of 1918 broke the party not only in the House of Commons but in the country. Local [Liberal] Associations perished or maintained a nominal existence. Masses of our best men passed away to Labour. Others gravitated to Conservatism or independence. Funds were depleted and we were short of workers all over the country. There was an utter lack of enthusiasm or even zeal.

## THE IMPACT OF THE WAR ON LLOYD GEORGE

Lloyd George's position underwent a real transformation after 1914. Some biographers have suggested that the 1914-18 war produced a hardening of Lloyd George's character and attitudes. His tendency to see issues in terms of black or white increased. It was true that he remained subtle, even sinuous, in his methods for resolving problems, but once he had made up his mind on the correctness of a given course of action he was extremely difficult to dissuade.

Before the war the prevailing view of him was as a radical, committed to welfare reform as a national priority, and willing to challenge the political establishment in pursuit of his goals. Despite the ministerial positions he had held, he could still be regarded as a political outsider with strong pacifist leanings. All that was changed by the war. From 1916, Lloyd George was Prime Minister of a predominantly Conservative Cabinet, wholly dedicated to the war and willing to shelve social reform for the duration of the struggle. On a *prima facie* judgement, it could be argued, as a number of Liberals did, that he had abandoned his earlier radicalism. There is some weight in this argument, but it has to be observed that Lloyd George's radicalism was never a set of fixed principles. It is unrealistic to expect any politician to be totally consistent in their behaviour. Circumstances constantly change; to remain effective a politician has to be prepared to adjust. A notable statesman of a later generation, Harold Macmillan, was once asked what he found to be the greatest problem in politics; he replied 'events', implying that no matter how consistent a line a politician may attempt to follow he is always to some extent at the mercy of happenings for which in the nature of things he cannot prepare.

Politics has been defined as the language of priorities. If this is taken as a working definition, it allows for a different interpretation of Lloyd George. The priority between 1914 and 1918 was national survival. He concentrated his attentions on tackling the huge problem that events had thrown up – the war. This diverted both him and the Liberals from the progressive policies they had followed since 1906. Lloyd George's very success in persuading many of his colleagues to accept increasing State intervention had the effect of diluting his own Liberalism and detaching him from the radical element in his party.

Conscious of this, at the end of the war, he made a number of important moves towards reconstruction. His aim was partly political in that he hoped to prevent the radicals from becoming too disgruntled over the slowing down of social reform. It was this that lay behind his 1918 election promise to make Britain 'a land fit for heroes'. The idea took particular shape with the creation of the Ministry of Reconstruction, which drew together the various committees that had come into being during the war, concerned with the improvement of standards of living and working. One notable product of this was the Education Act of 1918. This measure, which raised the school-leaving age to 14 and considerably extended educational opportunity generally, was largely the work of H.A.L. Fisher, a university vice-chancellor and one of the numerous non-political experts that Lloyd George had called into government.

## THE IMPACT OF THE WAR ON THE LIBERALS

The war had a number of adverse effects on the Liberal Party from which it never fully recovered. Although Asquith was replaced as Prime Minister in 1916, he continued as party leader, refusing to serve in Lloyd George's Cabinet; instead he led the parliamentary opposition. This anomaly meant that in effect the Liberals were divided from 1916 onwards between the Asquithians, who claimed to be the official Liberal Party, and the followers of Lloyd George. The Conservatives were bound to benefit from this split in the Liberal leadership.

They were also the direct beneficiaries of another major political consequence of the war. The coalition governments which first Asquith and then Lloyd George formed involved a governmental restructuring that resulted in Conservatives taking key executive posts in the inner Cabinet. Thus, without benefit of an election victory, the Conservatives found themselves in positions of authority for the first time since 1905.

By 1918, all the principal causes that had characterised pre-war Liberalism had been jettisoned or gravely compromised. Britain's entry into the war effectively ended the notion of the Liberals as a peace party, the economic regulation of the State by the wartime governments marked the abandonment of free trade. Conscription undermined the concept of the freedom of choice of the individual. The suspension for the duration of the war of the Home Rule Act, together with the Government's failure to achieve a satisfactory settlement in Ireland following the 1916 Easter Rising, appeared to leave the Liberals' Irish policy in tatters.

Furthermore, important though the play of politics at parliamentary and government level obviously was, attention must also be drawn on developments in the country at large. Historians have begun to stress the importance of what was happening at constituency level. On balance, the Conservative and Labour parties gained politically from the war, while the Liberals suffered. The main problem for the Liberal Party was that, although the majority of its members came to accept that the war was justifiable and therefore had to be fought to the utmost, it was hard to accommodate it easily within the Liberal programme as developed since 1906. Having struggled to establish the primacy of welfare issues, the Liberals now found themselves diverted from their social reform programme by the demands of war. Furthermore, having overcome the reactionary opposition of the Unionists on a whole range of issues before 1914, the Liberals now had to contemplate the prospect of their leaders making common cause with their political opponents. All this tended to take the heart out of party activists at grassroots level. Liberal morale sank. The Conservative Party was always less compromised than either the Liberals or the Labour Party. They had never had any doubts about the correctness of Britain's entry into the war. Their traditional claim to be the 'patriotic' party stood them well in wartime and led to a considerable recovery of popularity in the constituencies.

There is little doubt that Liberals lost irrecoverable political ground because of the war. Their traditional causes, defence, Ireland and electoral reform, were compromised. The existence of the Union of Democratic Control, representing the Liberals anti-war tradition, was a constant reproach to the Government. The Irish Nationalists felt betrayed by the Government's policy towards Ireland. Asquith was castigated for the British handling of the Easter Rising, as was Lloyd George for his use of the Black and Tans. The Irish Catholic vote in England switched significantly to Labour, while in Ireland the Nationalists moved into Sinn Fein (see page 99). In addition, Asquith, the official Liberal leader, remained highly unpopular over his continued resistance to female suffrage. To him it was not a matter of prejudice, but it resulted in a significant loss to the Liberals of women activists, a loss made worse by the increase in the number of female workers who joined the Labour Party following an agreement Labour made with the National Union of Women's Suffrage Societies.

An equally important factor accounting for Liberal Party decline was the electoral reform introduced in the last year of the war. The 1918 Representation of the People's Act swelled the number of voters from some 7 million to around 21 million. A number of historians, including Martin Pugh, regard this trebling of the electorate as having had momentous political consequences. Not all the newly enfranchised working class voted Labour in the 1918 election; nonetheless its share of the vote rose proportionally with the increase in the electorate from 7 per cent to 22 per cent and its number of MPs increased from 42 to 60. The inter-war trend towards the replacement of the Liberal Party by Labour as the second largest single party had been established.

In a notable book written in 1966, Trevor Wilson suggested that the war was the essential reason for the decline in Liberal fortunes. Other historians have queried this and have argued that the war accelerated the decline rather than causing it. Most recently Martin Pugh has suggested that the key factor is not so much that the war undermined the Liberals as that they failed to seize the opportunity that the war offered. Diverted by the demands of war from their reforming policies, the Liberals gave ground to the Labour Party as the new force of reform.

Whatever weight is given to the different interpretations, it is difficult to avoid the conclusion that the war was a highly formative experience in the history of the Liberal Party and indeed in British politics. The issue that commands attention is one of personality. Parties are not only about principles; they are also about people. The role of Asquith and Lloyd George is critical. Asquith's continuing resentment at what he regarded as Lloyd George's usurpation in 1916 meant that a genuine *rapprochement* between the two remained an impossibility. But the fracturing of the Liberal Party left Lloyd George dependent on the support of Bonar Law and the Conservatives. Whether this amounted to his being the 'prisoner of the Conservatives' is another of the lively debates among historians. It has to be said that contemporaries did not regard Lloyd George as a prisoner; they saw the Conservatives being dragged somewhat reluctantly behind this dynamic ex-Liberal leader.

| *timeline* | 1916 Dec | Conservatives withdraw support from Asquith, who resigns; Lloyd George becomes Prime Minister and forms new Coalition Government. War cabinet established with five members; Lloyd George, Bonar Law (Chancellor of the Exchequer and leader of the House), and Milner, Curzon and Arthur Henderson (Labour); Liberal Party in Parliament is split between the followers of Lloyd George, who receive the government whip, and the Asquithians, who claim to be the official Liberal Party. |
| | 1917 Feb | Russian Czar abdicates |
| | April | U-boat menace threatens Britain's life-line |

| Oct | Bolshevik Revolution in Russia |
| Nov | Formation of Supreme War Council |
| 1918 Feb | Representation of the People Act creates universal male and limited female suffrage. |
| May | Lloyd George survives the Maurice Debate |
| Nov | Armistice on the Western Front |
| Dec | Lloyd George and the Coalition Liberals win the General Election in alliance with the Coalition Conservatives – the 'Coupon Election'. |

## *Points to consider*

1) **Are there any grounds for regarding Lloyd George as having been a 'dictator' between 1916 and 1918?**
2) **Examine the links between the 'Maurice debate' in May 1918 and the 'Coupon Election' of that year.**
3) **How true is it to say that the 1914-18 war destroyed the vestiges of Lloyd George's radicalism?**
4) **Consider the view that by 1918 the Liberal Party was in a state of irreversible decline.**
5) **Were the Liberal divisions that developed during the war more a matter of personalities than of principles?**

# 9

# LLOYD GEORGE AND THE COALITION, 1918–22

## DOMESTIC AFFAIRS

Reconstruction which had begun during the war was continued into the post-war period. A massive demobilisation programme, involving the return of over one million men to civilian life, was set in motion under Winston Churchill's direction. Ambitious proposals were drawn up for improved health facilities, unemployment pay and pensions. The grim economic circumstances in post-war Britain, caused by high inflation and declining orders for British goods, largely thwarted these schemes, but there was notable success in regard to housing. Under the Addison Act of 1919 over 200,000 council dwellings were built between 1919 and 1922. Throughout the Coalition years Lloyd George continued with his aim of creating greater co-operation in industrial relations. He maintained links with both employers and trade unions and sought to encourage them to think in terms of conciliation rather than confrontation.

Unfortunately, these successes were overshadowed by the larger drama of the postwar breakdown in industrial relations. It was coal mining that attracted the greatest attention. Coal, once one of Britain's staple exports and the basis of her nineteenth-century industrial strength, was becoming increasingly difficult to mine profitably. The wartime blockade of Britain had greatly reduced foreign orders, which were not renewed after 1918. In addition, even the most sympathetic capitalist found it difficult to speak well of the obstinate mine owners. The miners unions' demanded that the industry, which had been brought under government control during the war, should not be returned to the owners: mining should be re-nationalised. Lloyd George was unable to satisfy them on this; neither could he sanction government interference in order to meet the miners' wage demands. He was able, however, to use his negotiating skills to defuse the situation in 1921 when it appeared likely that the railwaymen and transport workers would join the miners in a general strike. However, the embers of syndicalism had been fanned in the South Wales coal fields and the Coalition had to face continuing unrest and disorder there and in the industrial areas of Britain that were suffering from the post-war economic recession.

It was Britain's inability to cope with the effects of the worldwide industrial slump that undermined Lloyd George's promise that the workers of Britain would be well rewarded for their heroic wartime efforts. By 1922, unemployment had risen to over one million, inflation had leapt ahead of wage levels, and the existing social services were stretched beyond their capacity. Worse still, by 1922 the economic situation had become so bad that the Government, rather than expand social welfare provision, had to cut back. The withdrawal of resources, known as the 'Geddes Axe', after Sir Eric Geddes, Chairman of the special government-appointed committee which recommended them, applied to education, hospitals and housing. All governments tend to be judged primarily in relation to their economic record. The evident failure of the social and economic policies of the Coalition tended to dwarf its successes in other spheres. The mistakes seemed too many, suggesting that the problems of post-war Britain had proved too great for Lloyd George's government to cope with effectively. Even an apparent social-policy success such as the Addision Act brought it little public approval, since the measure was thought not to go far enough and any real improvements were attributed to the Labour controlled local councils, who were largely responsible for implementing the policy.

## FOREIGN AFFAIRS

Lloyd George had conducted an ill-advised 1918 election campaign in regard to Germany. He had to a considerable extent succumbed to the prevailing anti-German hysteria in promising to treat the defeated enemy with great severity. This flew in the face of his own better judgement and the reality of the situation. As he showed at the Versailles peace conference, where he tried to hold the balance between the idealism of the USA and the chauvinism of France, he believed that it made no sense to impose a humiliating peace settlement upon Germany. He was opposed to heavy war reparations being demanded from Germany and he argued against too much territory being taken from her. He described the maintenance of future peace in Europe as 'dependent upon there being no causes of exasperation to the vanquished which will leave them violently seeking redress' and warned the Allies that nothing was more calculated to bring about a new war 'than that the German people should be surrounded by a number of smaller states each of them containing large numbers of Germans all clamouring for reunion'. He also prophesied, accurately as it turned out, that the victor nations would be unwilling in the future to risk war in defence of an unjust treaty.

Despite his status as a world statesman being confirmed by his diplomacy at Versailles, Lloyd George had only partial success in his negotiations. He was unable to prevent swingeing reparations being imposed on Germany or to stop the forcible incorporation of a number of German peoples into neighbouring foreign states (see map on page 97). The Peace Settlement of 1919 did not so much mark an agreement between the victors as a compromise between the French desire for revenge and the American concept of a just peace, with Britain somewhere in the middle urging moderation. The French preoccupation was with obtaining a settlement that would leave Germany so emasculated that she would never again be able to threaten France. But it was unrealistic to suppose that Germany could be left permanently weakened in keeping with French wishes. Britain had no wish to see Germany chronically disadvantaged. Quite the contrary; for Lloyd George the overriding consideration was that Germany be allowed to recover so as to provide a counterweight to French dominance in Europe.

In relation to the rest of Europe, Lloyd George's policy had greater success. Having earlier been an opponent of the new Bolshevik regime in Russia, established after the October Revolution in 1917, he showed considerable statesmanship in arranging a trade agreement between Britain and Soviet Russia in 1921 and preparing the ground for the international recognition of the new state. Unlike Churchill, who was an

*Germany after the peace negotiations in 1919*

ardent anti-Bolshevik on principle, Lloyd George had opposed the Russian revolutionaries solely because in November 1917 they had reneged on their alliance with Britain and France and had withdrawn from the war against Germany. Once Germany had been defeated, Lloyd George was prepared to be more understanding of the Bolshevik government. It is true that he had been responsible for the sending of British troops to Russia in 1919 at the time of the Civil War between the Bolsheviks and their enemies, but he claimed that it had never been Britain's intention to interfere in the internal affairs of Russia; Britain's only purpose was to recover the precious war materials she had previously shipped to imperial Russia.

## IRELAND

The Irish Treaty of 1921 represents arguably the outstanding success of Lloyd George's political career. To understand the importance of the

Treaty and the scale of his success, it is necessary to examine the nature of Lloyd George's involvement in the Irish question since 1916.

The suspension of the Home Rule Act at the start of the war had only shelved the Irish problem; it had not solved it. This became very apparent in April 1916 when a breakaway group of extremist Irish nationalists seized the General Post Office in Dublin and proclaimed the establishment of the Irish Republic. Although, after four days of bitter fighting, the republicans were overwhelmed by a British force and their ringleaders soon tried and executed, the Cabinet feared that this 'Easter Rising' might lead to further serious troubles in Ireland. Asquith turned to Lloyd George to find a solution. In a family letter Lloyd George commented wryly: 'Rather interesting that when there is a special difficulty they always pick on me'. He immediately entered into discussions with Redmond, the Irish Nationalist leader, and Carson, leader of the Ulster Unionists. Lloyd George's main objective was to prevent the Irish problem from undermining the British war effort. He confided to Carson:

> In six months the war will be lost . . . The Irish-American vote will go over to the German side. They will break our blockade and force an ignominious peace on us, unless something is done, even provisionally, to satisfy America.

In his urgency to reach a temporary settlement Lloyd George was not above giving contradictory promises to both Redmond and Carson, which persuaded them to accept a compromise, referred to as the 'Heads of Agreement'. This granted immediate home rule for the 26 counties of southern Ireland while the six counties of Ulster remained part of the United Kingdom until after the war, when their permanent constitutional status would be decided by an imperial conference. Lloyd George allowed Redmond to gain the impression that the separation of Ulster from the rest of Ireland was purely temporary; at the same time he reassured Carson that it would be permanent. However, Lloyd George's manoeuvring came to nothing for, when the Heads of Agreement were put to the Coalition Cabinet, the Unionist members refused to ratify it. They claimed Lloyd George had gone too far to appease the Irish nationalists. The most obdurate opponent was Lord Lansdowne, the leader of the Unionists in the Lords, who insisted that the Agreement be modified to accommodate Unionist objections. Asquith seemed unwilling to resist Lansdowne. When Redmond learned of this he broke off negotiations and the Agreement become a dead letter.

The breakdown of the negotiations over Ireland did not have the disastrous effects on the war effort that Lloyd George had feared, but it was now even more evident from the seriousness of the situation in Ireland that a solution had to be found. What Lloyd George had learned from this episode, and from the failure of an all-party Irish Convention set up by the Government in 1917, was that the Unionists were the major obstacle; if ever a workable settlement over Ireland was to be reached, it was they who would have to be won over or placated. This perception informed all Lloyd George's subsequent approaches to the Irish question.

Redmond's failure to achieve a settlement undermined the position of those nationalists in Ireland who believed that a peaceful solution was possible and put a great propaganda weapon into the hands of the extremists who argued that force was the only arbiter. The 80 Irish Nationalist MPs decided that they would no longer attend the Westminster Parliament. Notwithstanding this gesture of defiance, the Nationalist Party began to lose ground to the more extreme Sinn Fein ('Ourselves Alone' in Gaelic) Party, which had come to prominence in the 1914 crisis and whose leading members had played a major role in the Easter Rising. In 1917, the year in which Eamon de Valera became its leader, Sinn Fein won two by-elections. The British government's attempt to extend conscription to Ireland in 1918 only made matters worse. Despite being outlawed, Sinn Fein won 73 seats in the Coupon Election, seats which it pointedly refused to take up at Westminster. Instead, in 1919 it defiantly set up its own Dail Eireann (Irish parliament) in Dublin. In the same year Sinn Fein's military wing, the Irish Volunteers, reformed itself as the Irish Republican Army (IRA), dedicated to guerilla war against the British forces.

IRA activitists became so disruptive that Lloyd George sanctioned the recruitment of a special irregular force to deal with the situation; they were known from the colour of their uniform as 'Black and Tans'. The coercive tactics used by this force soon led to their being hated by Irish nationalists, who accused Lloyd George of employing them deliberately to terrorise the civilian population of Ireland. Indeed, Lloyd George was accused of applying the same methods in Ireland that 20 years earlier he had denounced as barbarous when used against the Boers. Critics were quick to draw attention to the apparent inconsistency between his advocacy of restraint in Europe and his employment of harsh methods in Ireland.

When it became apparent that peace could not be brought to Ireland by the use of military force, Lloyd George's thoughts turned again to the idea of a constitutional settlement acceptable to both Nationalists and Unionists. After decades of bitterness over Home Rule this would not be easy, but the atmosphere of the times encouraged change. The Versailles Settlement had enshrined the principle of national self-determination; it seemed anomalous that Britain, a victor nation and a signatory of the Versailles Treaty, should continue to deny that principle to Ireland. There was also the undeniable fact that Home Rule had been on the Statute Book since 1914; it was law, even though it had yet to be implemented. In addition, there were signs that the Conservative Party were ceasing to be as rigidly attached to the Unionist cause as they had been before 1914. They had grown weary of the strife in Ireland. It was also Lloyd George's view, as it had been Gladstone's, that had the Conservatives undertaken Home Rule it would never have encountered the resistance that the various Liberal Bills had.

Accordingly, in 1921 Lloyd George gathered together a team of negotiators that included the new Conservative Leader, Austen Chamberlain as well as Lord Birkenhead, previously one of the staunchest opponents of Home Rule. He then offered De Valera a truce and invited him and the other Irish leaders to London to discuss the drafting of a treaty of settlement. When they duly arrived, Lloyd George shrewdly played upon the idea that he represented the last hope of a just settlement for Ireland. He suggested that if they could not reach an acceptable agreement under his sympathetic leadership it might well be that he would have to resign, to be replaced by Bonar Law whose intransigence over Home Rule would destroy any chance of a settlement. His argument was persuasive enough to induce them to accept the appointment of a boundary commission charged with the task of detaching Ulster from the rest of Ireland. What this acceptance meant was that Irish nationalists had given ground on the critical issue; they had dropped their previous insistence that Ulster must be part of an independent Ireland.

With this as a bargaining factor, Lloyd George was able to convince the Unionists that the rights and independence of Ulster had been safeguarded. It was essentially the same position as had been reached in the 1916 negotiations, but on this occasion the Unionists did not scupper the talks. As Lloyd George had perceived in 1916, a settlement depended ultimately on Unionist acceptance. In December 1921, after a long, complicated series of discussions, in which all Lloyd George's arts of diplomacy, if not duplicity, were exercised, the parties finally signed the Irish Treaty, according southern Ireland Dominion status as the Irish Free State, with Ulster remaining part of the United Kingdom. In the event, the Treaty split the Irish parties and a savage civil war in Ireland broke out between the pro-Treaty Nationalists, led by Michael Collins, and the anti-Treaty Republicans led by De Valera.

In retrospect, the settlement of 1921 can be seen as both a remarkable historical achievement and a contemporary political failure. A British politician had had the vision, the skill and the luck to undertake successfully something which, since the 1801 Act of Union, had evaded all other politicians and statesmen who had approached it, a workable solution of the Anglo-Irish question. Of course, as subsequent events were to show it was far from being a perfect solution; nevertheless, judged against the scale of the problem originally confronting him, Lloyd George's achievement was prodigious. The political failure lay in the fact that the treaty was necessarily a compromise. The Unionists were left feeling betrayed by Lloyd George's willingness to give in to what they regarded as republican terrorisim. The Nationalists could not forget his use of the Black and Tans; nor could they regard the Treaty as anything other than a concession reluctantly and belatedly extracted from a British government who granted it only when all other means of maintaining the union had failed.

## THE FALL OF THE COALITION, 1922

One of the repercussions of Lloyd George's Irish policy was that it finally killed off the idea of a permanent coalition or centre party. To be workable this would have had to include Labour as well as Conservative and Liberal members. Notwithstanding the 1921 Treaty, Labour had found the methods that Lloyd George sanctioned in Ireland deeply distasteful and therefore unsupportable. It is doubtful in any case whether a genuine fusion of Liberal and Conservative was possible. At

Lloyd George's urging talks had been held between the Chief Whips of the Parties in 1920, but these had broken up with nothing substantial achieved. The fact was that Conservative support for Lloyd George was a matter of expediency, not principle; it did not imply any real desire to make that support permanent. The chances of a genuine coalition were always slim. Lloyd George did not really have enough to offer either the Conservative or Labour Parties. The atmosphere after 1918 was unsuitable; the Conservatives were too uncertain and Labour did not yet feel strong enough. They entertained thoughts of union only as a means of having a say in affairs until they felt sufficiently secure to strike out on their own.

After four years, the commonly held view of the Coalition was of a tired, ineffectual, administration, led by an individual who was past his best and was sustained in office by a combination of his own love of power and a Conservative Party that lacked the courage to attempt to take on the full responsibility of government. Commentators spoke increasingly contemptuously of the low tone of the Coalition, a reference to the unattractive mixture of economic incompetence, political expediency and financial corruption that had come to characterise it.

The charge of corruption took particular strength from the so-called 'Lloyd George Fund', which provided an easy target for those wanting to blacken his name. Unashamedly, Lloyd George had used his power of patronage as Prime Minister to employ agents to organise the sale of honours and titles on a commission basis. Maundy Gregory was the most notorious of these salesmen. It was said that the asking rate during the Coalition years was between £10,000 and £12,000 for a knighthood, and between £35,000 and £40,000 for a baronetcy. During this period some 90 peerages and 20,000 OBEs were purchased by well-heeled, if not always well-born, social aspirants. Lloyd George justified the practice by referring to the long tradition of patronage in Britain; the sale of titles, he suggested, was not new to British history. He argued that it was a justifiable means of raising political funds, given that he did not have access to the donations that the Conservatives regularly received from the business world or the Labour Party from the trade unions.

Whatever the validity of this claim, it did not prevent opponents from likening the honours sale system to the pre-war Marconi scandal as yet another example of Lloyd George's dishonesty. It provided a powerful additional argument for those Conservatives who had begun to question their party's continued support for Lloyd George. They pointed out that that support had always been conditional and suggested that the corruption of the Coalition, added to its failure in domestic, economic and foreign policy, was now beginning to taint the Conservative Party itself.

More substance was given to their complaint by the Chanak affair. This was a crisis arising from the resentment of the defeated Turks at the dismemberment of their country under the terms of the Peace Treaty of Sevres (1920). Under their new leader, Mustapha Kemal (Kemal Ataturk), the Turks threatened to take back by force the territories they had lost to their old enemy Greece. Lloyd George, in the tradition of Gladstone, sided with the Greeks against their former oppressors. In September 1922 he ordered British reinforcements to be sent to Chanak on the Dardanelles, a likely area of confrontation. War threatened, but diplomacy eventually prevailed and the Turks withdrew. At home, Lloyd George's action was condemned by many Conservatives as an unnecessary and irresponsible piece of belligerence that might well have led to a major conflict.

Their chance to undermine him came shortly after, when Lloyd George announced his intention of calling a general election. This was now the moment for the Conservative Party to reappraise their relationship with Lloyd George: should they, in the light of the manifest unpopularity of the Coalition, continue to support him and it? In a decisive meeting of the party, held at the Carlton Club in October 1922, the Conservative MPs voted by 187 to 87 to abandon Lloyd George and the Coalition by standing for election as a party in their own right. Stanley Baldwin, soon to be the leader of the party, joined Bonar Law in urging their colleagues to disassociate themselves from a Prime Minister no longer worthy of their trust. In an influential speech at the meeting, Baldwin spoke of Lloyd George as 'a dynamic force which had already shattered the Liberal Party and which was well on its way to doing the same thing for the Conservative Party'. The unpopularity of the Coalition and the political wisdom of the Conservatives' abandonment of it were shown in the results of the General election in November; which were devastating for the Liberals.

Lloyd George resigned following this overwhelming rejection. He was never to hold office again. The defeat marked the end for him as an executive politician and with it the end of the possibility, if not the

**TABLE 11**

| 1922 Election Result | Votes | Seats | % vote |
|---|---|---|---|
| Conservatives | 5 500 382 | 345 | 38.2 |
| National Liberal (Lloyd Georgians) | 1 673 240 | 62 | 11.6 |
| Liberal (Asquithians) | 2 516 287 | 54 | 17.5 |
| Labour | 4 241 383 | 142 | 29.5 |
| Others | 462 340 | 12 | 3.2 |

Electorate – 21 127 663      Turnout – 71.3%

notion, of developing an effective centre party in British politics.

The Coalition of 1918-22 has not had a good press. Emphasis has traditionally been laid on the apparent failures of Lloyd George's Government. It has been seen as an aberration in that it did not conform to the normal pattern of party politics. It is often suggested that by governing in peacetime without a genuine party majority, Lloyd George was doomed to eventual failure as 'the prisoner of the Tories'. His final defeat in 1922, following the withdrawal of Conservative support, is thus interpreted as in some way marking a return to normal two-party politics which had been disrupted by the war and Lloyd George's wish to perpetuate his own authority.

The objection to this line of argument is that it assumes that the two-party system is normal and necessary to British politics. What brought Lloyd George down was not his defiance of two-party politics, but the decision of the Conservatives to abandon him. Had it served their purpose to remain with him they would have done so. They were looking after their own interests, not defending some abstract political principle. Moreover, the notion of Lloyd George as their 'prisoner' was the interpretation of later observers. Few contemporaries saw it that way. Indeed, Martin Pugh has suggested that it suited the Conservatives after 1922 to portray Lloyd George as having been not their prisoner but as a dictator over them. In this way they were able to absolve themselves from the mistakes of the Coalition years.

|  | 1919 Jan | Paris Peace Conference begins. First Dail Eireann elected. Irish Free State proclaimed. Strikes in engineering industry |
|---|---|---|
| | Feb | Sankey Commission appointed into mining industry in order to avoid miners' strike. |

| | | |
|---|---|---|
| | Apr | De Valera elected President of Sinn Fein |
| | Aug | Sinn Fein declared an illegal organisation |
| | Sept | Railway strike. Dail prohibited; increasing violence by IRA |
| | Oct | End of railway strike |
| 1920 | Jan | Versailles Treaty comes into force |
| | Apr | Conscription ends |
| | June | Government recruits 'Black and Tans' to suppress IRA |
| | Oct | Miners' strike |
| | Nov | Miners' strike ends |
| | Dec | Government of Ireland Act passed |
| 1921 | Mar | Anglo-Russian trade agreement. Coal Mines denationalised |
| | Apr | Miners' strike. State of Emergency |
| | May | Elections to Irish parliament |
| | June | Miners' strike ends |
| | Oct | Conference to negotiate an Irish treaty in London |
| | Dec | 'Irish Treaty' signed, creating Irish Free State, excluding Ulster |
| 1922 | Sept | Chanak crisis |
| | Oct | Carlton Club meeting of Conservative Party votes to abandon their coalition with Lloyd George. Lloyd George resigns. Conservative Government under Bonar Law takes office |
| | Nov | General election returns Conservatives with substantial majority of 73 seats |

## *Points to consider*

1) How successful were Lloyd George's attempts at post-war reconstruction in Britain?
2) Why, in the post-war peace settlement, did Lloyd George advocate that Germany should be treated leniently?
3) Consider the proposition that the Irish Treaty of 1921 was both a 'remarkable historical achievement and a contemporary failure'.
4) How accurate is it to describe Lloyd George as 'the prisoner of the Conservatives' between 1918 and 1922?
5) Why did the Conservative Party finally decide to abandon Lloyd George in 1922?
6) To what extent does the Coalition of 1918-22 deserve the bad press that it has traditionally received?

# 10

# THE YEARS OF DECLINE, 1922–45

After 1922 the difficulty for Lloyd George was in determining what he and his shrunken band of followers actually represented. Since 1916 the Liberal wing that he had led had been defined by little more than loyalty to him personally, and the character of the Coalition between 1916 and 1922 was of personal rather than party government. That, indeed, was why the Conservatives chose in 1922 to detach themselves from it. Having tried unsuccessfully to fashion a third force in British politics, Lloyd George was reduced after 1922 to being the leader of a splinter group of a minority party, now second to Labour in terms of popularity. His past reputation would for some time continue to give him influence, but this was of a negative kind; Baldwin and Ramsay MacDonald, the respective Conservative and Labour leaders, remained fearful of him as a potential source of disruption.

In these circumstances, the only course of action was for Lloyd George to return to the official but much reduced Liberal Party. This duly occurred; at the end of 1923 he and Asquith agreed to forget their differences and reunite their followers in a single party with free trade as a rallying cry. The Liberal defence of free trade was not sufficient in itself, to make the Party electable, since that issue was ceasing to be the central national concern it had once been. It was given a lease of life only by Baldwin's clumsy attempt to make protection the main issue in a snap election in 1923.

The results showed some Liberal recovery, but it was the Labour Party's continuing growth that was more impressive. The Labour Party's showing in the election in the following year placed it in a strong enough position to form a minority government.

**TABLE 12**

| 1923 Election Result | Votes | Seats | % vote |
|---|---|---|---|
| Conservatives | 5 538 824 | 258 | 38.1 |
| Liberals | 4 311 147 | 159 | 29.6 |
| Labour | 4 438 508 | 191 | 30.5 |
| Others | 260 042 | 7 | 1.8 |

Electorate – 21 281 232     Turnout – 70.8%

**TABLE 13**

| 1924 Election Result | Votes | Seats | % vote |
|---|---|---|---|
| Conservatives | 8 039 598 | 419 | 48.3 |
| Liberals | 2 928 747 | 40 | 17.6 |
| Labour (LRC) | 5 489 077 | 151 | 33.0 |
| Communists | 55 346 | 1 | 0.3 |
| Others | 126 511 | | |

Electorate – 21 731 320     Turnout – 76.6%

By 1926, the year in which Asquith resigned as party leader, following Lloyd George's criticism of his lack of sympathy for the TUC's case in the General Strike of that year, the differences between the two Liberal factions had re-emerged. Lloyd George succeeded to the leadership but he inherited a party that had been decisively overtaken by Labour. He began to take an interest in economic theory as a way of restoring Liberal morale and appeal. A contemporary observed: 'when Lloyd George comes back to the Party, ideas come back'. Unfortunately, while this was certainly true, what the Liberals needed in the 1920 were not ideas, but leaders untainted by the ambiguities of their previous behaviour and a strong constituency organisation able to deliver the votes at election time. Lloyd George had never been particularly interested in the humdrum but vital concerns of party structuring. It was now too late. No matter what the quality of its political ideas may be, a party with no realistic chance of power, is not going to receive significant electoral support. By-election victories were not sustained in general election returns. 'A discredited down and out political adventurer' is how the Labour newspaper, *The Daily Herald*, described Lloyd George.

Nonetheless, he persevered. Influenced strongly by the idea of J. M. Keynes, the outstanding economist of his day, and formerly one of his severest critics, Lloyd George advocated a large-scale programme of government spending as a means of preventing further industrial decline. During the 1920s he wrote a number of books and articles in which he argued that unemployment could be overcome by government-sponsored public works. (His proposals were not dissimilar from those on which President Roosevelt was to base his New Deal programme in the 1930s). He introduced these ideas into the election campaign of 1929 but they made little headway with the voters. The Labour Party continued to outdistance the Liberals.

**TABLE 14**

| 1929 Election Result | Votes | Seats | % vote |
|---|---|---|---|
| Conservatives | 8 656 473 | 260 | 38.2 |
| Liberals | 5 308 510 | 59 | 23.4 |
| Labour | 8 389 512 | 288 | 37.1 |
| Communists | 50 614 | 0 | 0.3 |
| Others | 243 266 | 8 | 1.0 |

Electorate – 28 850 870     Turnout – 76.1%

Lloyd George stayed to lead the Liberals in the 1930s but he and they were a declining influence. Illness prevented his playing a direct part in the political reformation that occurred following Prime Minister Ramsay MacDonald's dramatic decision in 1931 to abandon the Labour Party and head a National Government made up predominantly of Conservatives. It was a remarkable echo of what Lloyd George had done in 1918. Lloyd George's subsequent decision not to support the National Government meant that in the following election he was left with only three supporters in the Commons.

His last major campaign carried the impressive title of 'The Council of Action for Peace and Reconstruction'. Promoted in 1935, it was a development of the Keynesian economic programme which he had adopted earlier. It won the support of a number of public figures, but significantly no politician of note could be persuaded to endorse it. Lloyd George's political influence was now only peripheral. The fragments of

**TABLE 15**

| 1931 Election Result | Votes | Seats | % vote |
|---|---|---|---|
| Conservatives | 11 978 745 | 473 | 55.2 |
| National Labour | 341 370 | 13 | 1.6 |
| Liberal National | 809 302 | 35 | 3.7 |
| Liberals | 1 403 102 | 33 | 6.5 |
| (National Gov't) | (14 532 519) | (554) | (67.0) |
| Independent Liberal | 106 106 | 4 | 0.5 |
| Labour | 6 649 630 | 52 | 30.6 |
| Communists | 74 824 | 0 | 0.3 |
| New Party | 36 377 | 0 | 0.2 |
| Others | 256 917 | 5 | 1.2 |

Electorate – 29 960 071    Turnout – 76.3%

the Liberal Party again reunited for the 1935 election but they made little impression on either the National Government or the Labour Opposition.

**TABLE 16**

| 1935 Election Result | Votes | Seats | % vote |
|---|---|---|---|
| Conservatives | 11 810 158 | 432 | 53.7 |
| Liberals | 1 422 116 | 21 | 6.4 |
| Labour | 8 325 491 | 154 | 37.9 |
| ILP | 139 577 | 4 | 0.7 |
| Communists | 27 117 | 1 | 0.1 |
| Others | 272 595 | 4 | 1.2 |

Electorate – 31 379 050    Turnout – 71.2%

Lloyd George's visits to the Commons became less frequent as he grew older. He spoke out against the foreign aggressions of Mussolini's regime in Italy and also against Hitler when the German dictator's malign intentions became clear. Unfortunately, Lloyd George had earlier thrown doubts on the quality of his own judgement when, following a meeting with Hitler in Germany in 1936, he had praised him as a far-sighted and creative statesman.

With the outbreak of war in 1939 Lloyd George showed that his skill as a parliamentary debater had not deserted him. His last contribution of note in the Commons occurred in May 1940 when he joined in the call for Neville Chamberlain's resignation. However, when Churchill took over as Prime Minister and suggested that he might care to consider a government post, Lloyd George declined. In January 1945, to the surprise of many of his former radical colleagues, Lloyd George accepted the title of Earl Lloyd-George of Dwyfor. This was three months before he died in March 1945. One form of epitaph on his career was the election result of that year, which confirmed the relegation of the Liberal Party to the fringe of British politics.

**TABLE 17**

| 1945 Election Result | Votes | Seats | % vote |
|---|---|---|---|
| Conservatives | 9 988 306 | 213 | 39.8 |
| Liberals | 2 248 226 | 12 | 9.0 |
| Labour | 11 995 152 | 393 | 47.8 |
| Communists | 102 780 | 2 | 0.4 |
| Common Wealth | 110 634 | 1 | 0.4 |
| Others | 640 880 | 19 | 2.0 |

Electorate – 33 240 391    Turnout – 72.7%

# REFLECTIONS ON THE LIBERAL DECLINE

Lloyd George's career after 1922 was reduced to reacting to events initiated by others. His past made him a figure who continued to attract attention, but although he was to influence events, he was never again to direct them. For a number of years the Conservative and Labour leaders treated him with some apprehension, but it became increasingly clear that his declining power base was reducing his effectiveness as a politician. Much has been made of the Liberal reunion in 1923, but this was little more than a desperate effort to close ranks in order to retain some vestige of political authority. His attempts to form a third party had represented his real hopes, but with the recovery of resolution by the Conservatives in 1922, there disappeared any real prospect of the coalition being developed into an identifiable and viable force in politics. Both Baldwin and Ramsay MacDonald were 'obsessed' with the fear of Lloyd George and had no genuine wish to work with him.

*Lloyd George and his wife, the Countess (formerly Frances Stevenson) in the last year of his life*

It is now evident that after 1922 Lloyd George's political career was one of steadily decreasing significance. He continued to produce proposals and ideas. He had much to say on unemployment and economic decline and addressed himself to the problems of international tension and rearmament. But Lloyd George's gifts were as a political practitioner, not a theorist. His reflections on politics were interesting, but they never had the impact or influence of those of Disraeli or Gladstone. One must not overstate the importance of this. In British politics, philosophy and theory seldom play a major part. British political development is essentially pragmatic. It is best understood as a series of reactions to events, rather than the shaping of things according to a set of predetermined ideas. That, indeed, is why the traditional Liberal Party had largely succumbed to the pressures of total war after 1914.

British political parties are themselves coalitions, held together by the hope of office. Unity and solidarity are often more apparent than real. The more radical a party claims to be, the more subject it is to division, since it is impatient for change. If a party finds itself in a situation where the prospects of office are remote, internal dissensions can soon surface, creating bitterness and recrimination. The reuniting of the Lloyd George and Asquithian Liberals in 1923 had been a papering over of the cracks, not a real unification. Asquith's leadership was hardly inspiring and he suffered in comparison with Lloyd George, who still maintained his dynamic public style.

On top of all this the Liberals were the victims of the imbalance of the British electoral system. This system had become more democratic in terms of those entitled to vote and stand for Parliament. At various key stages between 1832 and 1928 the franchise had been extended. By 1928 it was possible to describe Britain as having universal adult suffrage. However, a major anomaly remained. Although most of these measures had been accompanied by a re-distribution of seats and votes in order to keep constituencies roughly equal, no serious attempt had ever been made to introduce the principle of proportional representation (PR), that is, to allocate seats in accordance with a party's aggregate popular vote. The number of seats a party won was not determined by the overall number of votes it gained, but by the distribution of those votes within particular constituencies. The practice of 'first past the post' meant that large numbers of votes could be wasted by being bunched 'wastefully' in certain constituencies. This anomaly was not intentional, but had developed with the piecemeal and pragmatic growth of the electoral system.

It so happened that the Liberals were the party to suffer most from the perversity of the electoral system, whose inherent bias had begun to work significantly against them. As all the tables in this chapter show, the number of votes won by the Liberals was never proportionally represented by the number of seats gained. Aggregate support for the Liberal Party certainly did decline between the wars, but the real reason behind its loss of seats is that its votes were wasted by being concentrated unproductively in a limited number of constituencies. The irony was that in the cross-party talks which had preceded the drafting of the 1918 Reform Bill, the Liberals had firmly opposed the suggestions that the modified electoral system should include an element of proportional representation.

What also weakened the Liberals was that their previous record as a party of social reform made little impact between the wars. The economic depression of the inter-war years has tended to hide the achievements of the period. Historians now, however, are beginning to point out that while not as dramatic or as extensive as those of the pre-1914 Liberals or of the post-1945 Labour government, the reforms of the inter-war years did mark significant improvements in social welfare. Among the important developments were increased pensions, council-house building, maternity benefits and extensive electrification of homes through the national grid. These advances gave little opportunity for the Liberal cause to recover as there was nothing particularly distinctive that the Liberal Party had to offer that was not represented by the Conservative or Labour Party.

| timeline | 1923 | Lloyd George rejoins official Liberal Party *(60)* |
|---|---|---|
| | 1924 | His party is heavily defeated in the General Election that brings the Labour Party into office (January-October); General Election (November) Conservative Government formed *(61)* |
| | 1926 | Becomes Liberal Party leader again *(63)* |
| | 1928 | Publishes *Britain's Industrial Future* (the Yellow Book); Frances Stevenson bears him a daughter, Jennifer *(65)* |
| | 1929 | Leads Liberal election campaign under the slogan, 'We can conquer unemployment' *(66)* |
| | 1930 | Lloyd George-Ramsay MacDonald talks *(67)* |
| | 1931 | Liberals reduced to four seats; Lloyd George declines to serve in Ramsey MacDonald's National Government; Liberals split *(68)* |
| | 1932 | Liberals under Samuel reunite with Lloyd George Independent Liberals *(69)* |
| | 1935 | Bases his election campaign on a 'New Deal' policy of economic growth, but Lloyd George Liberals win only four seats *(72)* |
| | 1936 | Visits Germany; impressed by Hitler *(73)* |
| | 1937-39 | Attacks Neville Chamberlain's Government over its appeasement policy and failure to rearm *(74-76)* |
| | 1940 | Joins in parliamentary attack on Chamberlain over the Government's Norwegian campaign failure; declines invitation to join Churchill's Coalition government *(77)* |
| | 1941 | Death of his wife, Margaret *(78)* |
| | 1943 | Marries Frances Stevenson *(80)* |
| | 1945 | Created Earl Lloyd George of Dwyfor; dies on 26 March *(82)* |

*(numbers in brackets refer to his age)*

*Points to consider*

1) **What difficulties stood in the way of an effective re-unification of the Liberals after 1922?**
2) **Consider the notion that the disastrous 1945 election results for the Liberals formed a fitting epitaph on the political career of Lloyd George.**
3) **Was Lloyd George's career after 1922 simply a matter of living on past glories?**
4) **How much did the character of the British electoral system contribute to Liberal decline between 1922 and 1945?**

# 11

# LLOYD GEORGE AND
# THE LIBERAL DILEMMA

The rise of Lloyd George from relatively humble origins to the highest political office in the land was a remarkable achievement. It involved his breaking the mould of British politics. He defied a long-established tradition which dictated that only those from a particular social class and educational background could achieve political leadership. But the very fact that he reached such heights in defiance of political convention meant that throughout his career he never quite lost the image of an upstart. He was seldom fully trusted. Although in 1913 he was officially exonerated from the charge of impropriety over the Marconi scandal, the widespread belief that he had used his inside knowledge as Chancellor of the Exchequer to make a killing on the stock market dogged him for the rest of his career. Unfortunately, the suspicion with which he was regarded was as evident in his own Liberal Party as it was among Conservatives. The distrust was in part a reaction to his style of politics.

The scandals of Lloyd George's private life never became sufficiently public for them to destroy his political career, but they undoubtedly contributed to the image of him as being untrustworthy. This reputation had important consequences in foreign affairs. For example, his cloudy reputation had already preceded him when he entered the stage as an international statesman. His inability to impose himself more effectively on the deliberations at Versailles is explained in part by reference to his foreign counterparts' having already gained an impression of him as a dubious individual who needed watching.

The diary of Frances Stevenson and her correspondence with Lloyd George provides a remarkable insight into his technique as a politician. They confirm the picture of him as a charmer, a fixer, getting his own way more by cajolery and flattery than by simple power of argument. He believed that argument of itself seldom persuaded anyone. Playing upon self-interest was far more effective. That is why he appeared to excel in intimate political settings. It is true that he was one of the great parliamentary speakers and political orators of the modern age, but his greatest success as an administrative politician was gained from his use of the arts of persuasion in person-to-person contact. Although he excelled in the arts of 'politicking', his methods, whereby he brought in experts and interested parties, often took discussion out of the realm of formal party politics. Flexibility and adaptability came easily to him and throughout his career he made them his basic technique in discussion and negotiation. This often proved highly successful in resolving disputes and getting things done. The negative aspect of this was that he became regarded as a man who lacked principles.

In modern colloquial terms, Lloyd George was a hustler, a wheeler-dealer. It was frequently suggested that Lloyd George loved politics for its own sake, for the excitement that it brought, rather than because it offered a means of improving the public good. It was further argued that he was essentially power-hungry and that he used the Liberal Party merely as a vehicle for furthering his own ambitions.

Whatever the truth of that particular charge, it is certainly the case that his career fundamentally altered the character of the Liberal Party. He appreciated that 'party' was an unavoidable feature of the political structure, but he tried to move towards a position in which consensus politics would replace strict party alignments. His sympathisers have suggested that in this regard he was ahead of his time. They assert that because British politics had yet to outgrow the two-party system his approach was too radical for most of his less enlightened contemporaries who interpreted his attempt to reshape the political scene as essentially destructive.

The description 'socialist' was sometimes applied to Lloyd George. He always rejected the description; yet, judged purely in terms of the policies he followed it is sometimes difficult to see where he differed. Although he never openly acknowledged it, his work as a social reformer in the pre-1914 period was very much in tune with the programme of the

Labour Party of that time. His widening of central-government authority during the war extended the powers of the State to an unprecedented degree. Perhaps this is better described as socialism with a small 's', a means to an end, a particular response to a particular national crisis, rather than the acceptance of the political ideology implied by Socialism with a big 'S'.

In this respect it draws attention to the central dilemma created by the Liberal Party's attempt to modify its policies. Precisely because it was a halfway stage, the progressive but still limited form of social-service programme that the new Liberalism advanced was bound to be superseded by the full-blown welfare-state socialism of the Labour Party. Some historians have used this as the basic explanation for the decline of the Liberalism in the twentieth century. Thy have argued that the Liberal Party fell between two stools: in trying to be socially progressive it forfeited its claim to represent traditional values; however, despite its apparent radicalism it did not go far enough along the road of State control. It was thus unable effectively to challenge either the Conservatives, representing the force of tradition, or the Labour Party, standing for nationalisation and state-direction of the economy.

This is a powerful argument, but there are other considerations. As mentioned earlier, theory has been of only minor importance in British politics; historically, practice has proved far more significant. Party government in the twentieth century has been largely a matter of adapting to the needs of the time. Governments have behaved pragmatically rather than ideologically. This, indeed, has been a continual complaint of both the political Left and Right, who have wanted their respective parties to follow far more ideologically-based policies.

Contemporaries and later critics condemned Lloyd George for treating his party in so cavalier a way, as effectively to destroy it as a political force. Superficially the charge has some justification; it was during the most active period of his career that the Liberal Party declined in importance and therefore some of the blame must be attached to him. However, the charge of irresponsibility depends on an implicit acceptance of party interests as paramount. It assumes that a politician may not veer from his original political viewpoint without being judged guilty of betrayal or treachery. It is certainly the case that the adversarial character of British politics has always made it difficult for an individual to change parties without raising doubts about his political integrity. Few have made the change successfully. Those who do 'cross the floor' tend to be hated more by the party they leave than they are loved by the party they join.

Lloyd George remained in the Liberal Party throughout his political life, but he often found the restraints of party irksome. He accepted that party membership was a requirement of modern politics, but his attitude remained progressive. He was ahead of his time in believing that Britain's interests could best be served by pooling the best ideas, and not allowing artificial political barriers to prevent persons of competence working together in administration and in government, regardless of their political or social background.

It was often said of Lloyd George that he was the man who won the war. This is a reference, not merely to his ability to inspire the nation, but also to his success in preventing the generals from turning Britain into a military dictatorship. To speak of the power of the generals in such a way may appear extreme, but it is no less exaggerated to suggest, as some commentators have, that Lloyd George became a political dictator. The evidence offered in support of the charge of dictatorship is his neglect of parliament, his use of a personal secretariat and his technique of by-passing the normal channels in order to expedite his plans. The fact is, however, that the electoral structure in Britain prevented dictatorship. No matter how strong Lloyd George's authority may have appeared to be, he was always dependent in the final analysis on the continuing support of the Conservatives in Parliament. This was amply demonstrated in 1922 when his governmental power-base ceased to exist once the Conservatives chose to withdraw their support from him.

A persistent and disruptive influence in British industrial relations has been the notion of rivalry between capital and labour, employer and employee, as natural and therefore unavoidable. Lloyd George devoted much of his time to negotiating with bosses and workers, endeavouring to achieve settlements that were not simply compromises, but recognitions that employers, employees and government had a common interest. This ran counter to the Marxist principle which influenced even non-marxists, that relations in the economic sphere were necessarily confrontational. There are strong grounds for saying that it was Lloyd George who made the trade unions an integral part of British politics. His direct appeal to them in 1915 to suspend their agitation for the duration of the war and to enter into partnership with the Government was a recognition of their indispensability to the national war effort and gave the unions a consciousness of their status that they were never to lose.

Historians continue to debate and measure just how far war has been responsible for the changes that have occurred in British society in the twentieth century. Whatever view is taken, it is difficult to deny that the Liberal Party was greatly changed by its experience of war. To put it in negative terms, if the 1914-18 war had not intervened, Asquith might not have resigned, the Liberal social reform programme might have continued with Lloyd George as its main promoter, and the challenge to old Liberal values would not have reached the proportions that it did. Most of the signs indicate that the Conservatives, still wounded after their defeat over the People's Budget and the surrender of the House of Lords, would not have been able to oust the Liberals in the foreseeable future. Much of this, of course, is speculation. We cannot know what impact the Ulster question would have had on party strength and alignment had the war not occasioned the shelving of this issue, but it is highly improbable that the traumas and transformations experienced by the Liberals would have occurred without the pressure of the war years.

The importance of the war lies in showing that the Liberal principles were not absolute. DORA, conscription and the protectionist budgets of Lloyd George and McKenna proved this. Try as they might after the war, the Liberals could not return to their traditional values. This was only a short step from admitting that the values themselves were expendable.

A commonly held myth is that politics is about issues rather than personalities. However, it is observable in British history that great issues have invariably been associated with the individuals who represent them. It is impossible to separate the political questions of Lloyd George's time from the manner of their presentation and from the personalities of those who presented them.

An essential point to grasp about Lloyd George is that he did not have a political philosophy. He certainly had strong dislikes and firm opinions, but these do not necessarily constitute an idelogy in the sense of a structured programme founded on consistent attitudes. His Liberalism sat lightly upon him. He made politics a matter of personality.

There is a vital distinction to be made between Liberalism as a party political movement and Liberalism as a political philosophy. In many respects it can be shown that the latter kind of Liberalism, far from disappearing, survived to become the common outlook in Britain. Its biggest victory was in its impact upon the Conservative Party and the Labour Party. Each of these incorporated Liberal values into their respective conservative and socialist platforms and indeed into their political practice. This largely prevented the Conservative Party from moving to the reactionary Right and the Labour Party from shifting to the revolutionary Left. Both parties, for example, publicly espoused the need to preserve the rights of the individual while at the same time acknowledging the obligation of the State to provide for the welfare of all its citizens. This is another way of saying that British political parties share a common attitude towards major issues. It would be too much to suggest that this was exclusively or even largely the result of the career of Lloyd George. Nonetheless, it is possible to argue that his attempt at consensus politics and his achievements in coalition government, whatever their short-term failures or deficiencies, created a powerful precedent.

It has to be said that his readiness for compromise was not compatible with strong party loyalty and that as a consequence, the Liberal Party at a critical juncture in its history was irreparably fractured. Coalitions which appear to be maintained primarily in order to keep the Prime Minister in power are hardly calculated to strengthen party loyalty.

Therefore, it is difficult to deny that Lloyd George weakened the Liberal Party to the point of political impotence. At the same time, it is also arguable that he proved the most creative British politician of the twentieth century. He, more than any other single individual in British public life, laid down the basic political agenda for much of the rest of the twentieth century. The State as economic planner, the redistribution of wealth through taxation, social reform and the Welfare State, the acceptance of trade unions as part of the political and industrial framework: these have been the essential issues in British domestic politics in the twentieth century.

*Points to consider*

1) Was Lloyd George 'rooted in nothing'?
2) Did Lloyd George have any consistent political principles?
3) In political terms, which is the more appropriate description of Lloyd George, creator or destroyer?
4) How far is there a case for saying that Lloyd George was ahead of his time?
5) Consider the view that the real measure of Lloyd George's political significance is his impact not on the Liberals but on the Conservative and Labour Parties.

# BIBLIOGRAPHY

Of the many studies of Lloyd George the following are recommended to students keen to develop their understanding of the man and his times. The list includes the major writers and works referred to in Chapter 3.

Paul Adelman, *The Decline of the Liberal Party, 1910-1931*, London 1986. An informed survey of the many theories relating to Liberal decline.

John Belchem, *Class, Party and the Political System in Britain, 1867-1914*, Oxford, 1990. A Historical Association booklet, intended to introduce students to the main issues regarding party development in the period.

Peter Clarke, *A Question of Leadership; From Gladstone to Thatcher*, London, 1991. Contains many interesting observations on Lloyd George as Liberal leader and Prime Minister.

Stephen Constantine, *Lloyd George*, London, 1992. An informative essay on Lloyd George, concentrating on his role as a social reformer.

George Dangerfield, *The Strange Death of Liberal England*, London, 1970. First published in 1935, this is a seminal work that established the terms of debate on the decline of Liberalism.

Bentley Brinkerhoff Gilbert, *David Lloyd George, a Political Life*, London, 1987 and 1992. A massive study of the subject, the book is still in progress and so far has reached 1916 with volume II.

Martin Gilbert (ed.), *Lloyd George*, New Jersey, 1968. A collection of key documents, with a very useful introduction by the editor.

John Grigg, *Lloyd George*, London, 1973-85. Another huge work, on the same scale as Bentley Gilbert's; so far three volumes have appeared, covering Lloyd George's career up to 1916.

Elie Halevy, *The Rule of Democracy, 1905-14*, London, 1951. Although written in the 1920s, this work by a great French historian, remains an excellent introduction to the study of pre-war Liberalism.

Judith Loades (ed.), *The Life and Times of David Lloyd George*, Bangor, 1991. A collection of eleven excellent essays by leading scholars on key aspects of Lloyd George's career.

G.I.T. Machin, *The Liberal Governments of 1905-15*, Bangor, 1991. A short and very up-to-date treatment of the Liberals in power.

Donald McCormick, *The Mask of Merlin*, London, 1976. Controversial, hostile to its subject, but worth consulting as an example of the fierce reaction that Lloyd George is still capable of arousing.

Ross McGibbon, *The Evolution of the Labour Party, 1910-24*, Oxford, 1974. Makes very good reading on the relations between Lloyd George and the Labour Party.

David Marquand, *The Progressive Dilemma: from Lloyd George to Kinnock*, London, 1991. Has much of interest to say on Lloyd George's contribution to British party politics.

Kenneth O. Morgan, *Consensus and Disunity, The Lloyd George Coalition 1918-1922*, Oxford, 1979. A detailed examination of Lloyd George's last years in power.

Kenneth O. Morgan, *David Lloyd George, 1863-1945*, Cardiff, 1981. A short entertaining biography by a leading authority and prolific writer on Lloyd George.

Kenneth O. Morgan (ed.), *Lloyd George: Family Letters, 1885-1936*, Cardiff, 1973. Well worth consulting for its revelation of Lloyd George's public and private concerns.

Frank Owen, *Tempestuous Journey*, London, 1954. A sympathetic view of Lloyd George's rise to the top.

Henry Pelling, *Popular Politics and Society in Late Victorian Britain*, London, 1968. One of the many books by an outstanding analyst of the period.

Martin Pugh, *Lloyd George*, London, 1988. An up-to-date biography that takes in all the important modern research on Lloyd George.

Donald Read, *Edwardian England, 1901-15*, London, 1972. Particularly good on the pre-war crisis in Britain.

Peter Rowland, *Lloyd George*, London, 1975. A detailed and critical study of Lloyd George.

Duncan Tanner, *Political Change and the Labour Party, 1900-1918*, Cambridge, 1990. An important analysis of the rise of the Labour Party and the decline of the Liberals.

A.J.P. Taylor, *Essays in English History*, London, 1974. Contains two vital essays for students of Lloyd George: "Politics in the First World War" and "Lloyd George: Rise and Fall".

A.J.P. Taylor (ed.), *Lloyd George: a Diary by Frances Stevenson*, London, 1971. Gives many insights into Lloyd George's private life and political career.

A.J.P. Taylor (ed.), *Lloyd George: Twelve Essays*, London, 1971. A collection of studies by various scholars on a variety of central themes.

A.J.P. Taylor (ed.), *My Darling Pussy: The Letters of Lloyd George and Frances Stevenson*, London, 1975. Their intimate relationship in their own words as well as a series of insights into the politics of their time.

John Turner, *British Politics in the Great War: Coalition and Conflict 1915-18*, London, 1992. A recent re-examination of a critical period in Lloyd George's career and in British party politics.

Trevor Wilson, *The Downfall of the Liberal Party 1914-35*, London, 1966. An important work which set the pattern for analyses of Liberal decline.

Chris Wrigley, *Lloyd George* Oxford 1992. An important biography by a leading authority on the period.

Note: Students are strongly urged to visit the Lloyd George Museum in Gwynedd, North Wales. Built on the site of Lloyd George's boyhood home in Llanystumdwy, near Criccieth, this museum contains a large collection of documents, photographs and films tracing the rise of David Lloyd George from Welsh politician to international statesman.

*Appendix 1*

# SYNOPSIS OF LLOYD GEORGE'S CAREER

Lloyd George's career can be broken down into a number of identifiable periods:

**1890-1905**  These were his early years as a young Liberal MP, espousing Welsh causes and making a name for himself as a radical attacking the landlords and arguing for the disestablishment of the Welsh Church. He became a nationally known figure with his withering onslaughts on the Unionist Government for its mishandling of the Anglo-Boer War (1899-1902). He added to his reputation by vigorously defending free trade against the protectionist policies advanced after 1903 by Joseph Chamberlain and the Conservatives.

**1905-14**  This was his great period as a social reformer. As a dynamic member of Asquith's pre-war cabinet, first as President of the Board of Trade and then as Chancellor of the Exchequer, he was responsible for promoting a whole range of measures that marked the first steps towards the welfare state. His 1908 introduction of old age pensions was followed a year later by the so-called 'People's Budget' which threatened to undermine the landed class by the introduction of a tax on land. The dispute that this started reached its climax with the bitter clash between Lords and Commons over the Parliament Bill in 1911, the same year in which his National Insurance Act was introduced.

**1914-16** Holding in turn the offices of Chancellor of the Exchequer, Minister of Munitions, and War Secretary, Lloyd George made a major and dramatic contribution to the organisation of Britain's war effort.

**1916-18** In a highly controversial episode Lloyd George took over from Asquith as Prime Minister in December 1916. During the next two years he committed his inexhaustible energies to the defeat of Germany. In leading the nation to victory he fought a series of running battles with the politicians and the generals. He made enemies but his immense personal contribution was an undeniable factor in Britain's survival and success. He was widely accepted in Britain as 'the man who won the war'.

**1918-22** Lloyd George continued as P.M. at the head of a peacetime coalition government, a decision which widened the growing split in the Liberal Party. He added to his renown as an international statesman by personally leading the British delegation at the Versailles Peace Conference in 1919. Another outstanding achievement in this period was his presiding over the negotiations that led to the signing of the Irish Treaty of 1921, the nearest that any single politician has come to solving the Anglo-Irish question. However, his attempts to fulfil his wartime promise to make Britain 'a land fit for heroes' made little headway. Growing domestic problems and increasing disenchantment with Lloyd George led the Conservatives, the main prop of the Coalition, to withdraw their support from him in 1922. This effectively ended his premiership. Lloyd George was never again to hold office.

**1922-31** The split in the Liberal Party seriously weakened it as a political force and enabled the Labour Party to take over as the principal parliamentary opposition. The Asquithian Liberals and his own followers formally reunited in 1923, but it was not until the death of Asquith in 1926 that Lloyd George became the leader. He attempted to reinvigorate the Party and win back the lost Liberal voters with a set of policies aimed at tackling the great economic problems of the day. Despite such efforts and the impact Lloyd George made personally, the Liberals could not recover the lost ground; they were superseded as a radical party by Labour which formed minority governments in 1924 and 1929. There were expectations that Ramsay MacDonald, on breaking with his former Labour colleagues in 1931 to form the National Government, would invite Lloyd George to join his new Cabinet. But Lloyd George's serious illness at this time and his dislike of MacDonald killed such ideas.

**1931-45**  The twilight years – Lloyd George continued to contribute energetically to the national debates on the great issues of the economy and foreign policy, but the continuing decline in electoral support for the Liberal Party meant that he was never again in a position which allowed him to put his ideas into practical effect.

# GOVERNMENTS DURING LLOYD GEORGE'S POLITICAL CAREER

| | Party in Office | Prime Minister |
|---|---|---|
| 1886-92 | Conservatives | Lord Salisbury |
| 1892-95 | Liberals | W.E. Gladstone, *1892-94* |
| | | Lord Rosebery, *1894-95* |
| 1895-1905 | Conservatives | Lord Salisbury, *1895-1902* |
| | | A. Balfour, *1902-05* |
| 1905-15 | Liberals | H. Campbell-Bannerman, *1905-08* |
| | | H.H. Asquith, *1908-15* |
| 1915-18 | Wartime Coalition (Libs/Cons/Labour) | H.H. Asquith, *1915-16* |
| | | D. Lloyd George, *1916-18* |
| 1918-22 | Peacetime Coalition (Cons/Lib/Labour) | D. Lloyd George |
| 1922-24 | Conservatives | A. Bonar Law, *1922-23* |
| | | S. Baldwin, *1923-24* |
| 1924 | Labour | J. Ramsay MacDonald |
| 1924-29 | Conservatives | S. Baldwin |
| 1929-31 | Labour | J. Ramsay MacDonald |
| 1931-40 | National Government | J. Ramsay MacDonald, *1931-35* |
| | | S. Baldwin, *1935-37* |
| | | N. Chamberlain, *1937-40* |
| 1940-45 | Wartime Coalition (Cons/Labour/Lib) | W. Churchill |

# INDEX